PSYCHODRAMA EXPLAINED

OTHER BOOKS BY SAMUEL KAHN

PSYCHODRAMA EXPLAINED

by

Dr. SAMUEL KAHN

With an introduction by
Dr. *J. L. Moreno*

PHILOSOPHICAL LIBRARY
New York

INTRODUCTION

1302173

Dr. Samuel Kahn, the author of *Psychodrama Explained*, is one of the most interesting psychiatrists I have met in the course of my travels through the United States and abroad. His wide and varied interests are solidly founded on extensive studies that gained for him both the M. D. and Ph.D. degrees. He is an encyclopedist versed in the fields of psychiatry, sociology, psychology, education and music therapy.

But the basic drive in his life, the focal point of his unselfish devotion to his profession, is his eagerness to help the mental patient or student of any variety. One must admire Dr. Kahn's simplicity as a man, his common sense, his character and integrity, and his wisdom and experience as a clinician.

During more than thirty years of practice, Dr. Kahn's personal contacts have brought him a nation-wide following. Once an individual or a family has entered into contact with this warm and sensitive man, they never forget him; they always come back to him. They follow him wherever he travels, from Croton-on-Hudson, where he has established a dynamic therapeutic community, to Florida or the West Coast. He is an ever-active, ever-moving dynamo, available day and night to his patients whenever they call upon his help. May sound like a fairy tale, but it is a true portrait of Dr. Kahn.

This book is another illustration of his eagerness to study new methods such as psychodrama and group psychotherapy, so that he can try them and use them for the benefit of his patients. I am certain that the reader of this book will become acquainted with the ideas underlying the psychodramatic method, and will be stimulated to look into the broad literature of the field for further information. I hope, too, that the reader will be stimulated to visit Training Institutes where psychodramatic methods are used both for the treatment of the mentally ill and as a prophylaxis for those who crave to understand their own problems and the problems of others.

Psychodrama can be effectively used as a form of group psychotherapy, but is by no means restricted to this application. The method is widely used, both in the United States and abroad, by psychiatrists, psychologists, sociologists and educators, wherever human relations are studied. The flexibility of the method allows it to be used by itself, or in combination with other psychotherapeutic methods. Psychodramatic techniques can be used in counseling, and in reverse role playing aimed at exploring social problems, business problems, and personality situations.

J. L. MORENO, M.D.
MORENO INSTITUTE
Beacon, N. Y.

CONTENTS

PSYCHODRAMA EXPLAINED

PSYCHODRAMA: INTRODUCTION AND OVERVIEW

Psychodrama is a form of psychotherapy in which the participants enact, or re-enact, situations that are of emotional significance to them. The word *psychodrama* was coined by Dr. J. L. Moreno from the Greek words *psyche,* meaning mind, or soul, and *dram,* meaning to do or to act. In combination, these two words mean the expression of an individual's intellectual and emotional processes, not only through speech, but also through movement and gesture. Psychodrama is usually a group activity (though in certain cases the group may consist of the minimum number of two — a therapist and a patient), and is best carried out in a theater specially designed to facilitate certain therapeutic techniques.

One patient, or a group of patients, act out on the stage their "private personalities" and the personalities of other people in their lives, under the guidance of a director who is also a therapist, and in the presence of an audience composed of other patients. An actor is not restricted to acting out his own personality and feelings. In the course of enacting a particular incident he may find that another person in the scene (representing, perhaps, a boss, teacher, parent or sibling) is out of character; in such cases the main subject may *show* just how that parent or sibling does in fact behave, by temporarily taking the role himself. The audience is by no means a passive collection of spectators; any member may find himself taking part in the action, either spontaneously, at the request of one of those on the stage, or by the director.

1

In the course of playing these various roles the participants obtain insights into their own personalities, into some of their problems, into their own psychological workings, and into their own feelings and those of others. Strong emotions may be released, from which no participant (unless he deliberately cuts himself off from what is going on around him) is entirely immune. Insights are not confined to patients; in the course of a psychodrama the director himself, or his assistants, frequently recognize certain of their own problems, patterns of behavior, or motives; and this recognition may help them to solve or handle their own problems. For this reason psychodrama need not be confined to groups of people whose problems are pathological — it is basically a training in acting out past and present problems, both realistically and symbolically, both alone and with others, and develops a spontaneity and awareness from which perfectly normal people can also benefit. Nobody is without fears, personality weaknesses and anxieties of some kind; nobody is perfectly understood by himself or others, nor is his understanding of other people complete. But every person who acts out parts of his life on a psychodramatic stage finds that in some measure he becomes better understood. Equally, he acquires a deeper understanding of himself and others, so that he can direct more of his emotional energy toward finding satisfactory solutions to his daily problems, thereby relieving some of his tensions and anxieties.

Before discussing the specific techniques of psychodrama, it may be useful to consider briefly some of the changes that take place in an individual's thinking and behavior when he merges with others in a group, and particularly to note some of the differences between psychoanalytic theory and psychodramatic theory as they relate to groups.

a) *The Psychoanalytic Viewpoint.* Freud and his co-workers were primarily interested in individual psychology, and for the

2

purpose of gaining a better understanding of the mental processes underlying the behavior of the individual they formed two functional constructs of the psyche, or mind. In one of these, the psyche is divided into the unconscious, the pre-conscious, and the conscious. The unconscious is, as it were, the storehouse of everything the individual has ever experienced, but the information it contains is not available to the conscious mind. At this level, the individual wishes, but does not recognize his wishes. Freud likened the pre-conscious to an antechamber with a door to the unconscious and a door to the conscious. Thoughts, impulses, desires, crowd to the inner door, but there is an imaginary "censor" which allows only certain of them to penetrate the antechamber. Once there, these thoughts, memories, dreams, or desires are available to the conscious mind, but only if its attention is drawn to them in some way — and this is not a voluntary process. In the second construct, which in some sense overlaps the first, the psyche is divided into the id, the ego, and the superego. The id (very roughly) corresponds to the unconscious, and is the source of all the emotional energy available to the individual. The ego combines parts of the conscious and parts of the pre-conscious; it is the source of our sense of identity, and among its functions is that of reality-testing. The superego is, one might say, a combination of a hero of our childhood and an admonitory parent, which has a permanent place in our personality and exercises a considerable degree of control over the realization of the reality-based decisions of the ego.

In *Group Psychology and the Analysis of the Ego* (published by Boni and Liverwright, New York, 1921) Freud compares individual psychology with social or group psychology. He states that individual psychology is primarily concerned with the individual man, who seeks and explores the paths that will lead to satisfactions for his instincts. Yet we know that an individual is inevitably involved with, or influenced by, other people. His

3

relationship with them is on the one hand group involvement, and on the other hand his perception of them in the roles of model, love object, helper or opponent, is part of his private mental life. Individual psychology is, therefore, at the same time social psychology. Freud goes on to enumerate some of the relationship involvements of an individual, and how profoundly he is influenced by parents, siblings, love objects, teachers, companions, physicians, and even the imaginary characters of literature. Although some persons may be more narcissistic and more withdrawn than the average (the type which Bleuler called "autistic") it is very seldom that one finds a person involved *only* with himself.

In explaining his views on group psychology Freud elaborates on these considerations, pointing out that any person who has at some time been organized into a group for a specific purpose is deeply concerned not only with himself as an individual, but with his membership of his race, nation, profession, institution, or even of a crowd in which he finds himself, unless he is extremely regressed. Freud is then led to consider the possibility that there may exist an instinct which may be called a social instinct, herd instinct, or group mind, and claims that the "social instinct" is really derived from the family.

Dr. Le Bon, in his famous work, *The Crowd*: *A Study of the Popular Mind* (12th ed., Fisher Unwin, 1920) describes the most striking characteristic of a psychological group as follows:

. . . whoever may be the individuals who comprise it, however like or unlike by their mode of life, their occupation, their character, or their intelligence, the fact that they have been transformed into a group puts them in possession of a sort of collective mind which makes them feel, think, and act, in a manner quite different from that in which the individual would feel, think, and act, were he in a state of isolation.

4

There are certain ideas and feelings which do not come into being, or at least are not transformed into action, except in the case of individuals forming a group. Any psychological group is a potential entity, composed of heterogeneous elements which temporarily combine as cells do, and which, by their union, constitute the body of a new being that displays characteristics very different from those displayed by any of its component cells in isolation.

There is a certain resemblance between the characteristics of neurotic behavior in the individual, and the behavior of a crowd. People who exhibit neurotic behavior are guided more by what is *psychologically* real to them (pathologically distorted though their perceptions may be) than by *objective* reality. For example, an hysterical symptom may be a reaction to phantasy accompanied by a sense of guilt, rather than to real experience; and some forms of obsessional neurosis may be based not upon fact, but upon an evil intent which was never carried out. Similarly, experiences in dreams and under hypnosis, though frequently delusional and hallucinatory by objective standards, are nevertheless psychologically real to the dreamer. In this sense, the mental operations of a group exhibit some of the characteristics of neurosis, and in particular, a crowd's capacity for reality-testing is disproportionately small compared to its energy and desires with their affective cathexis.

As soon as a certain number of human beings, or indeed of animals, are gathered together, they tend to place themselves under the authority of a chief. The group, therefore, may be regarded as an obedient herd which cannot live without a master. Its members have a thirst for obedience, and submit themselves to any individual among them who boldy proclaims himself their master. To retain the leadership, this individual must believe strongly in what he is doing, and have personal qualities that enable him to awake similar faith in the group members, so

5

that he can impose his will or induce them to submit their will to his. Such a leader and his ideas have an irresistible power over others, which may be called prestige.

Prestige is a domination exercised over a group by an individual, a work, or an idea; it paralyzes the group members' critical faculty and fills them with astonishment and respect. But prestige is retained only so long as it brings success to the whole group; it is lost when failure creeps in. Politicians who understand that prestige can create a collective inhibition of intellectual functioning in a group, or heighten its affectivity, may have an enormous success with their voters. Further, prestige can be transferred from the leader to the group itself. Social groups possess a prestige proportional to the prestige of their leader, and function (at least in part) like a collective mind of great power and influence. Individuals of the group mind are highly suggestible to the ideas of other members, especially those of the leader, and are ready to sacrifice themselves and their ideas in the collective interest; they can also create a kind of contagion that will induce others to attach themselves to the group.

It seems that in the functioning of a group mind, the conscious personality of each individual disappears, and the unconscious personality takes over, permitting a kind of contagion of feelings and ideas. The partial disappearance of the conscious personality is accompanied by a corresponding relaxation of normal inhibitions and restraints, so that in a mob these ideas can easily and quickly be translated into action. This is particularly the case when there is a vocal and persuasive leader, and may result in killing, as in the recent Birmingham disaster and other lynchings. It is important to remember that a group, being strongly influenced by the unconscious, is impulsive, changeable, and irritable. Reality and consequences are not as important to the group mind as to the individual mind. The conscious

6

mind constantly weighs evidence and makes at least some use of the intellect in determining a course of action. The group mind, on the other hand, has little critical faculty. The ego and superego are forgotten, and the logic of the group mind is based not on the intellect, but on the associations of the id as they arise — and is therefore almost unpredictable in its course. The feelings of the group are always primitive, simple, and very exaggerated — a previously existing slight antipathy or suspicion can rapidly be converted into raging hatred. A group mind functions, to some extent, in many sociological activities of life, and its effects are seen particularly in war, religion, politics, and advertising.

b) *The Sociological Viewpoint.* Trotter, in *Instincts of the Herd in War and Peace* has suggested that the tendency to form groups is biologically an extension of the multi-cellular character of all the higher organisms. Whether or not this is so, the fact remains that every man spends his entire life as a member of one or more sociological groups. He has no choice. The infant could not survive outside the family group, in isolation, and it has become more and more difficult for an adult to isolate himself — and indeed, even if it were possible, such an adult would be something less than human, being deprived of the opportunity to develop many of those qualities that particularly distinguish humanity. Man he would remain, perhaps even physically perfect man, but an imperfect human, nevertheless.

The first sociological group experienced by any person consists of the minimal number of two — mother and child. And this relationship, as it develops, has an enormous influence on the development of the child's modes of interacting with other individuals in later life. The growth of the child is characterized by the constant enlargement of the scope of his relationships, both in number and in depth. The first stages of this enlargement take place within the family; from the one relationship with his

7

mother, he proceeds to develop relationships with the other members of the family. Then the scope is enlarged by contacts with individuals outside the family, and the child becomes aware of common ties between his own family and neighbors by reason of religion, national or regional customs, and special ideas or interests. And by the time the individual has grown to adulthood he finds himself a member of many large and small groups; in some of these (nationality, religion, ethnic group), his membership is by birth; in others it is by his own choice. But he wants to belong; it is safer to belong to a group than to be excluded, and being left out brings with it fears and insecurities very much like those of the "separation complex." When he is finished with one group he joins others, if he is normal. Inferiorities, fears, phobias, compulsions, insecurities, separation, rejection, isolation and loneliness are all deviations. Man may transfer from one group to another, but belong to a group he must, whether in social exchanges, in business — or in therapy.

c) *The Psychodramatic Viewpoint.* Unlike psychoanalysis, which is primarily a therapy of the individual through the *verbalization* of emotions, psychodrama is a therapy of the group through the *enaction* of emotions, and encompasses not only words, but also movement, gestures, at times even dancing and song. There need not be detailed analysis of the individual's psychological personality, for the dramatizations help to produce a group mind, in whose functioning the salient psychological traits and motivations of each individual are revealed. In the group minds, completely contradictory ideas can exist side by side without any conflict arising from the logical contradiction. In this respect the life of the group is similar to the unconscious mental life of children, some adults, some neurotics, and most psychotics. We should remember that in young children quite opposite attitudes can exist side by side, without logical conflict and without interfering with each other. At one moment the child will

8

love with all his heart, and almost at the same time he will express great hatred. And his feelings of love and hate may be displaced or projected upon someone else. As he matures emotionally, he becomes able to identify these emotions and give them their logical place. And once again, it is well to remember that neurotic motivations are determined by the psychological reality of the individual, which may be quite divorced from objective reality.

There are many possible motivations for joining a psychodrama group, ranging from an intellectual desire to learn the techniques in order to become a therapist, to an intense fear of being institutionalized or of shock therapy which persuades a disturbed individual that psychodrama is a preferable alternative. A normal person who functions well both socially and emotionally may join such a group as a means to deeper self-knowledge. Many people are convinced that psychodramatic experience will make them more efficient, and this is often the case, especially if they have a good psychological or psychiatric background. Even if they have not, it is highly probably that they will obtain insights into their motivations and emotional functioning, that will enable them at the very least to find a direction in life and to increase their skill in human relationships.

I mentioned that the dramatizations help to produce a group mind. In view of the characteristics of the group mind described above, one might reasonably question whether this is desirable. But it should be remembered that in a psychodramatic session there is a trained director, whose main function is to control and direct into constructive channels the emotions that are unleashed. Because the group is relatively small, it does not have at its disposal the emotional and physical energy of a large mob; further, the very suggestibility inherent in group mind functioning not only works toward translating emotion into action,

9

but facilitates the control exercised by the director. The individual does not have the same consciousness of self in the group that he would have if he were thinking out the problem alone, but there is still some self-consciousness which, under the guidance of the director and in the presence of the audience, results in the retention of self-respect and in the elimination of extreme hostility and violence. It is the task of the director, who is usually a psychiatrist, a psychologist, or a therapist, to maintain a degree of emotional freedom that will permit catharsis and the obtaining of insights, while restraining extremes of behavior. Before describing the techniques by which these results are obtained, I should like to consider some characteristics of drama and dramatization, since these play such an important role in the therapy.

d) *The Drama.* The drama is that body of literature which presents the emotional problems of human life in a form suitable for interpretation to the audience by live actors. There is a double imitation, here. The composer of the drama creates a set of characters who think, feel, and act in imitation of live human beings. The drama can, in the written form, convey to a reader the emotional makeup of the characters to such an extent that he can reasonably predict how they would behave in situations other than the one presented by the dramatist. But a far more potent emotional impact is made when these characters are imitated and interpreted by live actors on a stage before an audience. Each of us desires to experience the feelings and concepts involved in being human. We can express thoughts and emotions through speech, gestures, movement, dance, song, silence, pantomime, and these actions are learned in society from others, either in normal social intercourse or from the ceremonial and ritual attached to joyous or solemn occasions. Aristotle remarked that we instinctively imitate others from infancy onward, and that this imitation gives us learning, perception, in-

10

sights, and pleasure. Any assumption, in a role, of a character other than our own, is a form of drama. When professional imitation extends into action, there is strong drama. *But there is no drama without imitation.*

Most nations have dramatic literature, which varies in some of its characteristics from nation to nation. English and American dramas, for example, contain far more speech than Indian and Chinese plays, which rely heavily on song, dance, and pantomime. There was a strong religious influence running through the Egyptian dramatic literature. But in all cases the central theme is presented in terms of action through imitation. The author, within the framework of the tastes and tendencies of his age and the current theories of aesthetics and morals, empathizes with and interprets a human problem. There has been plenty of theorizing on the nature of the drama, yet no dramatic theory has ever given rise to a single dramatic work of lasting value unless the creative force was there to animate the form. And this creative force is not in the subject of the drama, but in the dramatic idea of action.

In concluding this section, I would say that every dramatic action must have an internal unity. In psychodrama, we find that people's actions and thoughts function in unity because they have mental patterns, chronic attitudes, and behavior patterns, which are identifiable and whose consequences are predictable. Just so, in the stage drama, we have a unity in the chain of cause and effect that derives from the psychological makeup of the characters. The stage drama borrows the laws of life, and translates them into action in an emotionally exaggerated fashion. Most dramas include both normal and neurotic patterns of thoughts, the normal and the abnormal, fears, hostilities, revenge, compulsions and obsessions, good characteristics and bad — all fitted into a tight, united structure for the purpose of presenting

11

the essentials of a cross-section of life. The structure itself imitates life, too, with climaxes and anti-climaxes, suspense, anxieties, distractions, and comic relief. But the drama, in its imitation of life, makes its impact because of the compression of time and the selective exaggeration of the emotions. This characteristic has great relevance to the psychodrama, too, as we shall see later.

e) *Psychodrama: The Stage and the Characters.* Although a stage is not absolutely necessary, the psychodrama is best performed in a special setting. The two best psychodrama theaters known to me were both designed by Dr. J. L. Moreno, and are located at the Government Hospital, St. Elizabeth's, Washington, D. C., and at Dr. Moreno's own sanitarium at Beacon, New York. The main feature of these theaters is the special stage, accessible from all sides by means of three broad and circular steps. These steps form a connecting link between the subject and the other participants, and the audience, and have additional psychological significance during the process known as the warmup, of which I shall say more in another chapter. The stage itself is circular or elliptical. At the Beacon theater there is also a gallery at a little distance from the stage, and a balcony towards the front of the stage itself. The balcony is reached by a flight of steps and is available to the subject and the other actors, though in fact it is not often used. Opposite the balcony, at floor level, is the control board for the lights. Dimmers permit the director to mix the available colors and regulate their intensity, so that he can to some extent set the emotional tone of any scene by the effect of the lighting.

The *spectators* sit in front and back of the stage, and are usually pulled into a group by the director, instead of being allowed to spread out in isolated clumps or individuals. At the psychodrama theater of the Moreno Institute in New York City, when there is a large audience, it is possible to seat spectators around three sides of the stage — in this theater there is not enough room for seating at the rear, though the two steps run all the way round the stage and may be used by the actors. The audience is much more than a passive collection of spectators. They look on at the action taking place on the stage, and during the action the part they play is limited, but they nevertheless have an important role in the total effect of the psychodrama.

The *director* is usually a psychiatrist, a psychologist, or a psychotherapist. In the early stages of the psychodrama he selects, from the material presented by the subject (either in private or in group), a scene which can readily be acted out. In the later stages he is constantly on the lookout for clues to the subject's feelings, and guides, rather than directs, the action into scenes that he feels may help the subject by giving him either catharsis or insights into his own feelings, or both. It goes without saying that the director, whatever his professional occupation, must be an individual who is sensitive to the subject's feelings and can understand the meaning of the non-verbal, as well as the verbal communications that constantly take place.

The subject, or *protagonist* as he is called in the psychodrama, in acting out scenes from his life, reveals both to the director and to the spectators many thoughts and feelings which may have been deeply repressed. The entire purpose of the psychodrama is to bring these thoughts and feelings into the light of day so that the protagonist may take a look at them and find that they are neither so unique nor so terrible as he may have thought. They are part of him, to be acknowledged as current facts about him. And since the action is entirely imitation of real life, the protagonist finds that he is not restricted to reproducing scenes as they actually did occur; he

13

can re-enact them to show what he would have wished to happen. Many individuals suffering from stagefright, or from feelings of inferiority, bring panic in their train; many, too, have real, imaginary, or borrowed feelings of guilt that make them unable to talk about themselves. The setting and the techniques of psychodrama do much to open them up, to free them. In particular the physical motion that is encouraged by the director has a loosening effect on nearly everyone, and it is not uncommon to find even the most blocked individual becoming more verbal under the influence of the action. Some mental patients act out their hallucinations and delusions, and in their movements and physical responses, as well as in their words, are contained many clues to the underlying causes of their problems.

So far we have mentioned other participants, but have said little about their roles. The director may call upon anyone present at the session to become an *auxiliary ego,* that is, an actor who plays the part of a person of importance to the protagonist. Such an actor is called an auxiliary ego because he is, in some sense an extension of the protagonist's ego. The role he plays represents the facet of the real individual which impinges on the protagonist; the director may even play the role of the protagonist himself, as a kind of mirror in which the protagonist can see for himself how he acts and speaks in a given situation.

There is also a special kind of auxiliary ego known as *the double.* The double is the inner, hidden personality of the protagonist. Sometimes the double appears when the protagonist, after a scene, speaks aloud the thoughts and feelings that it has aroused in him. Sometimes, when he finds it difficult to do this, or even to express his true feelings during a scene, the double, who is also an auxiliary ego, stands behind the protagonist, imitating his actions, and also speaking aloud the thoughts which are present in his mind but which he himself is afraid to voice.

Psychoanalysis uses free association and dream interpretation to bring about both catharsis and insight; psychodrama uses the total individual as he moves and speaks on the stage. The movement tends to produce a growing spontaneity in the protagonist, so that he becomes able to act roles other than his own, to "put himself in someone else's shoes," in fact, and through this process to understand their feelings in encounters of which he had previously understood (very imperfectly) only his own part. The protagonist also plays reverse roles, in addition to his own. Thus, if the actor playing, say, the protagonist's father, does not impart the right feeling tone to the scene, the protagonist may switch roles and play his father while an auxiliary ego takes the protagonist's role temporarily. This role-reversal often leads the protagonist to a completely new understanding of the dynamics of a scene, as well as showing the director and spectators just how the father appears in the subject's eyes. This appearance may not correspond to objective reality; it is, nevertheless, psychological reality for the subject.

Thus, the psychodrama attempts to synthesize psychological analysis with dramatic action, and to build a living picture of the protagonist's private world with all its prejudices and fantasies. In making this picture clear to the protagonist himself, it frequently develops his intuitive and creative abilities, as well as giving unlimited opportunity for reality-testing in a very protected situation.

f) *The Variants and Aids.* Because the psychodrama aims at creating and re-creating the psychological reality of the patient, the emotional tone of a scene is of the highest importance. Any medium or device that will help the patient to perceive and to express his emotions in action is, therefore, useful to the director.

15

I have already mentioned colored lighting; music, too, is a powerful stimulus to the evocation of emotion, and may be used as such on the psychodrama stage, either alone or so that the patient can express his feelings through the motions of the dance. Hypnosis and religious ceremony or ideas can also be used in combination with the dramatic action for building up the physical body, and for helping to solve certain problems connected with body-concept. Physical exercises and bodily positions may be used effectively for special effects. Where the spontaneity induced by role-playing would be of help in solving business and social problems that do not involve deep feelings nor require painful insights, modified psychodramatic techniques may be employed to highlight the issues involved, rather than the emotional and "depth" thought-processes of the individual's thinking part.

This form of group therapy is now widely used in public and private hospitals, clinics, and colleges. Many new ideas and techniques have been worked out in recent years; however the original techniques developed by Dr. Moreno are still basic to the art of psychodrama. He takes the position that the patient must act out the different roles and situations that are in his mind. In his actions and words, the patient discovers how he feels and how the other members of his family feel. As a dramatist, he is urged to make free use of gesture and movement, and to say and do what he wants. He is encouraged to re-live on the stage the painful and pleasurable experiences he has known; to experience them both as they were and as they might have been or might still become; and to learn from these re-creations new and more rewarding ways of responding to situations. The only restrictions placed on him in his search to know who and what he is and might be, are the minimal ones necessary to avoid danger to himself and to the others who share his explorations. At times "brain storming" is used.

16

The Place of Psychodrama in the Psychotherapeutic Scene

The psychotherapeutic scene is quite startling in the number and diversity of the methods used to induce behavioral and attitudinal changes in persons whose personality makeup is such that (for whatever reason) they find it difficult or impossible to function adequately within the current framework of their society. Among the methods added frequently to psychodrama are chemotherapy and supportive treatment, counseling and guidance in various forms, the production of sociological and environmental changes, suggestion (including religious ceremonies, autosuggestion, and hypnotherapy), removal from environment, change of occupation, physical exercises with or without dietary treatment and the use of analytical and group methods. In general, however, there are some broad classifications of dualistic or multitudinal approaches which apply to nearly all methods of treatment. One possible dichotomy is between the physical and the psychological methods; another is between directive methods, in which the therapist *interprets* the patient's dreams and behavior, and the non-directive in which he only *mirrors* the patient's feelings and attitudes; yet a third is between methods in which the primary emphasis is placed on the individual's unconscious drives, and those in which the emphasis is on the external influences.

Group psychotherapeutic methods are to be found on both sides of most of these dichotomies, of which the last is perhaps the most important for the purpose of this volume. It is the dichotomy between the emphasis on the individual per se and the emphasis on the group that differentiates two of the most

17

important methods currently used: psychoanalysis and psycho-drama. Both of the methods originated in Vienna before World War I, Freud being the pioneer of psychoanalysis and Moreno the pioneer of group psychotherapy and psychodrama. Although many practitioners of psychoanalysis also use group psycho-therapy quite extensively today, the dichotomy still holds good. The psychoanalytic practitioner treats the individual *in* the group — Slavson, for example has said: "By and large, it is an error to speak of the group as an entity in therapy. It is always the individual, and not the group as such, that remains the centre of the therapeutic attention."*

Moreno and Frieda Fromma-Reichmann, on the other hand, have pointed out that when action brings the world into the therapeutic situation, the group, as a miniature society, mirrors the society of the larger world. The psychodrama is a group effort to help an individual, but it is also a psychodrama of our culture, pointing up not only where the individual has failed to contribute to his society, but where the society fails to help the growth of the individual.

And there is one further sharp dichotomy between the psy-choanalyst and the psychodramatist. The former restricts his communication with the patient to the verbal level, and regards any attempt by the patient to act out his feelings as a form of resistance. The psychodramatist, by contrast, regards acting out as an effective means of dissipating and removing resistance to the therapeutic process.

This is not to say that psychodrama rejects all the Freudian concepts. On the contrary, like every school of psychotherapy and counseling, psychodrama owes an enormous debt to the discoveries of Freud. It is mainly in the application of these

* Slavson, S. R. *An Introduction to Group Therapy,* New York, The Commonwealth Fund, 1943.

18

concepts that the two schools diverge. Freud, although he wrote about group dynamics, leaned heavily on individual dynamics to provide an explanation of the behavior of large and small groups. Moreno, in his writings, places far more emphasis on the special dynamics of the group as a social force, and on the importance of society and the individual's role in society as forces acting upon the individual.

Much of Moreno's strength stems from his concept of spontaneity, which is developed in the subject by the role-playing techniques and particularly by the technique of role-reversal. These techniques frequently bring to light the neurotic or psychopathological implications in the behavior of both the protagonist and the other actors. In the psychodrama both the actors on stage and also the audience frequently exhibit a remarkable degree of therapeutic insight, and the insights are conveyed in a manner that enables them to be integrated and put to practical use in real life. It is in this sense that everyone present at a psychodrama is an active participant.

Role-playing provides a bridge to unite the family background with the individual's life experiences from infancy onward. The matrix of identity between these influences is existential, but not necessarily experienced, so that in the individual's life there are various stages of development in attitudes, which converge and are unified in the whole series of his roles, beginning with the physiological and psychosomatic roles which are manifested as social roles. The other roles — the sexual role, the role of the sleeper, eater, dreamer — are all tied together and integrated into a social self, which can be exhibited as a psychodramatic self. In other words, there are a number of elementary selves which finally add up to the social self, the "I." Imbalance in any one of these roles may produce disturbances of the total self.

The total self is a comparatively late development. In his

infancy the individual does not at first differentiate between himself and others, or between himself and objects. Gradually, however, as differentiation takes place, the individual finds himself playing an increasing number of roles, to each of which different psychic experiences are attached. And if any one of these roles is imperfectly developed or experienced, the individual's behavior in this area is deviant and may show pathological characteristics. These characteristics become very evident in the course of his role-playing on the psychodramatic stage in which he imitates and reproduces his behavior in relation to society.

Abnormal roles are intervening role fragments which are alien to the individual and are manifested in neurotic or psychotic behavior. Roles may be partially developed, normally developed, or overdeveloped. The absence of one or more roles in the individual is manifested in indifference, withdrawal, inactivity, or lack of reactions. Such a missing link may also be characterized by hostile or bizarre behavior. Overdevelopment of certain roles may produce equally deviant behavior. The origins of over- or underdevelopment of important roles may lie far back in the individual's childhood, where the deviation originally occurred as a defense against intolerable painful or threatening situations or thoughts. However, where these reactions persist into quite different situations, to which they are not at all appropriate as neurotic or pathological defense mechanisms, seen in so many so-called normal people. They show up very clearly in psychodrama — often far more clearly and quickly than would be the case in a purely verbal form of therapy — and from watching the defenses used by a subject in his role-playing on the psychodrama stage one may estimate his possibilities and future behavior.

THE PSYCHOSOMATIC PICTURE

Neurotic behavior can be rather loosely defined as behavior based upon a psychological reality that does not correspond to the objective reality of the patient's environment. Now, if we look closely at the people around us, we shall find that every single one of them shows some degree of neurotic behavior. (It is normal to be a little abnormal.) Of course individual people differ vastly in the degree to which their psychological reality differs from the objective reality, and also in the extent to which they translate this difference into action. But I would go so far as to say that some degree of neuroticism is inherent in the human condition; a complete absence of neurotic traits is almost inconceivable and would be quite as abnormal as functioning that is almost entirely neurotic. (Perfectionism is neurotic.)

One reason for the existence of "normally neurotic" behavior is the close interrelation between bodily functioning and mental functioning. We may, for example, become irritable and upset to a degree out of all keeping with the objective reality of a situation, because we are at that time suffering from some physiological disturbance. Pre-menstrual tensions in women can produce such behavior — the tensions have an organic cause, and also tend to cloud the sufferer's perception of reality, so that her behavior appears erratic. Conversely, conflict and anxiety that have a purely psychological basis may manifest themselves in the form of headaches, spastic pains, or allergic reactions — all psychosomatic symptoms.

It is, therefore, extremely important to know whether a patient's symptoms have a physical basis which can be treated medically, or whether they are predominantly psychological in character.

Some of the commonest neurotic symptoms that appear to some degree in normal people, and to a far greater degree in neurotics are: inferiorities, superiorities, doubts, ambivalences, compulsions, obsessions, inhibitions, hostilities, sadism, masochism, hypersensitivity, ignorance, superstition, fanaticism, fixations, narcissism, poor intelligence, blocking out, lack of interest in oneself and others; improper attitudes towards parents, authorities, siblings; jealousies, improper identifications, abnormal emotions, anxieties, excessive fantasizing, use of many escape mechanisms, overeating, oversleeping; insecurities, both real, imagined or borrowed; tension headaches; various spastic pains, which may be displacements as the result of functional conflicts; etc. It must be remembered that not all headaches are functional, as conflict and anxiety headaches. There are many other causes of headaches, such as various infections, tumors, hypertension, kidney and other diseases, sinus or eye infections, traumas, allergic reactions, cerebral hemorrhage, poisons, teeth, throat, ear, and other infections and referred pains, nicotine and food poisoning, anemia and other blood conditions, malignancies, etc.

If there are indications for referral to medical, surgical, or laboratory men, or special psychologists, or to psychiatrists for consultations, diagnosis or treatment, the referral should be made as soon as psychotherapy is started, or very soon after. Suspected psychotics should be referred to psychiatrists, severe neurotics to psychoanalysts, and people without medical problems can be referred to psychologists, psychoanalysts, or psychodramatists. If these people have already consulted some of the specialists mentioned, they can be referred to a different type of specialist for re-evaluation and for further results.

Then the various psychological, medical, physical and laboratory tests, should be carried out, including the accepted intelligence, personality and other psychological tests. The frustration level can also be ascertained by tests like the Rosensweig. Good personality tests are Rorschach, T. A.T., Sentence Completion, etc. For adults there are many good intelligence tests, most of which contain modifications of the Binet Simon, Terman, or Wechsler tests. The Blackie, Wisc, and other similar intelligence tests are better suited to very young children. The author's Directed Nonsense Test is new and very valuable for getting a quick short view of the individual's unconscious (the testee must first learn how to talk Directed Nonsense).

Anxiety hysteria or anxiety reactions are very common, and may lead to or be accompanied by other symptoms. Anxieties are frequently treated medically with sedatives, tranquilizers, endocrine products, trips, religion, athletics, changes of jobs, etc. But such treatment attacks only the symptom, without discovering the real cause of the anxieties. Some of the underlying reasons may be found through psychodrama, psychoanalysis, psychological guidance procedures, or discussion with family members who may know the person thoroughly. It is seldom that anxieties exist alone without other symptoms. People who harbor anxieties may show psychosomatic symptoms with obsessions; neurasthenia and hysterical symptoms with phobias; and all kinds of defense mechanisms, which are seldom understood by the patient himself. He may depend upon medicine to quiet him but this will not teach him the cause of his troubles and how to handle them. Many anxieties have their real origin in the unconscious, and the causes are deeply repressed and forgotten. Sometimes the causes of the anxieties may be acted out on the psychodramatic stage and they may be understood by the protagonist or director.

Usually phobic and anxiety-ridden patients who suffer with these symptoms for long periods develop panic attacks, and then seek help. The emergency may be a panic attack which may force the patient to seek immediate help by going into an institution, to a psychologist, psychiatrist or a psychodramatist.

At the first interview, whether the patient is anxious or appears relaxed, he must be received with interest and calmness, patience and understanding. Above all, the therapist should appear neither alarmed nor indifferent. If the medical examination has shown nothing of a serious nature, the patient should be told this fact; he may be told that there is nothing *physically* wrong with him, but not that there is nothing wrong with him, for a functional symptom is a real symptom. Let us repeat: he should not be told that there is *nothing* wrong with him. Such a statement will not help him at all, and is obviously untrue. His symptoms may be largely imaginary, but they are *real to him*. If he thinks he needs some kind of therapy, therapy is what he should get, even if it is limited to mild sedatives and warm baths, which often are of great help in bringing the patient to a state where more tangible help can be given him. During this preliminary period of treatment the therapist's observations of the patient will usually suggest to him what line of approach would be most fruitful.

The psychodramatist may not be the person to whom the patient initially went for help. In that case, he will conduct his own first interview, in order to get as much of the patient's background as possible. Many of the questions will be repetitions of those which were asked by the medical practitioner who made the referral, or by the specialists who conducted the physical examination. The repetition in itself is unimportant, but the patient's reaction to it may be revealing. In any case, the psychodramatist cannot depend upon second-hand information; he must "size up" the patient himself.

The patient is watched for what he says, how he says it, what he has left out, his facial and muscular expressions, color of skin, salivation or dryness of mouth, blocking, eagerness to cooperate, emphasis, the way he carries himself, his attitude, etc., all of which may help in making a tentative diagnosis, even before he reaches the psychodramatic stage. The patient should do most of the talking, while the therapist should be a good listener and take mental or written notes, particularly of the complaints and whatever other clues can be discovered. At times clues may be pieced together from the fragments of the interview. There should be no arguments, guilt giving or threats. The therapist should look for personal, family, schooling or occupational problems, and obtain family, personal, physical, mental, scholastic, occupational and social histories. This history-taking may continue for a few visits, when necessary, during which time the patient's physical, mental, and social maturities may be assessed.

Some people give their histories willingly, while others feel that they are being cross examined by a "district attorney" and accept the burden of proof upon themselves to prove themselves innocent. With this attitude, they may give an inaccurate account, either by withholding some facts, twisting other facts, or by just not answering some questions or blocking them out.

In the case of quarrels between husband and wife, the husband usually gives one story, while the wife will give different facts. There are also differences in the facts given by parents and their grown up children.

History taking must be done with gentleness and tact. However, the truth must be obtained in some fashion. Therefore, the interviewer must try to get the real facts, which means that although the interviewer uses tact, he must not be shy or bashful about obtaining the essential facts, even if it requires

25

a number of interviews to do so. But it must also be remembered that the patient may actually not know the answer to a question, because of a poor memory, misinformation, or not understanding.

The history of a neurosis will show a gradual development of symptoms, whereas a history of a psychosis may show a sudden onset of symptoms. Yet if the interviewer looks carefully into the history, he will find neurotic or even psychotic symptoms, long before the outbreak of a full fledged psychosis. Psychotic symptoms may be present one day, and then subside and be pushed into the background, until something triggers the symptoms again.

The beginnings or onset of hysteria, anxieties and phobias should be gotten, if possible, and the conditions under which these symptoms started; how often were they repeated, what caused them to subside, and what situation aggravated them? Who else in the family or among the friends had similar symptoms? Many patients will deny or belittle these symptoms, which are important, while exaggerating other symptoms, which may have little bearing on the case.

If the patient came voluntarily for help, he will be more willing to give an accurate history. If he was forced to come for therapy, his history may not be as accurate. Voluntary patients come for treatment when they have experienced or are experiencing a crisis, or when they are in trouble. Marital differences, quarrels between parents, school troubles, business and other problems, and jail threats, are some of the crises which may send people into treatment. Neurotics present themselves for treatment more often than psychotics. Organic conditions are less frequent than functional conditions. Functional neuroses are more common among the people who ask for treatment, but the most common symptoms are found in organic cerebro-arterio sclerotics.

26

If there appears to be a good rapport between interviewer and patient then the questions can be more pointed. Strong attachments, both positive and negative, to one or more individuals, to one or more objects, should be noted, and the relationships. This knowledge will enable the interviewer to know whether a transference or "tele" can be established to the therapist. In other words, if there is a history of abandonment, no attachments, negativity or withdrawal, it may be difficult for the patient to transfer, or he may become negative toward the therapist. The right kind of attachment may help to determine the prognosis, if regular sessions and treatment can be arranged. If the history gives a poor object attachment, and if the therapy is not regular, the prognosis may be poor.

Do not force the patient to tell all of his history in the first interview, in case he feels embarrassed. If he is pushed too much, he may not return. If he voluntarily talks, listen to all he has to say. Do not promise a cure, or he may become discouraged if it does not take place quickly. Also do not leave the patient in the air about his condition.

He should, instead, be told that improvement in his condition will be the result of his cooperation with the therapist. The working out of his problems will be a joint effort.

Questions about his sexual history may be asked in the first interview and perhaps in the second or third, if he will cooperate. Do not push it at first, if the patient seems reluctant to talk about it. You may be able to get other parts of the history later on. If the patient does talk about masturbation, do not hesitate to get detailed facts as to his age at its beginning, regularity of its continuation, when last performed, under what conditions, and the various methods performed. The fantasies under these conditions are frequently quite revealing. With the masturbation history, it is also important to find out about

27

thumb sucking, playing with breasts and with the rectum, hair, nail biting, sniffing, ticks, and other mannerisms. Some females imitate the male in their masturbation, and some males imitate the female. These all have meaning, if they can be associated with the fantasies. It is also important to find out whether the fantasies have a sadistic or a masochistic character. Interviews are best carried out in private.

Watch for blushing, shyness, seclusiveness, hostilities, jealousies, various fears, various forms of narcissism, homosexual thoughts, hostility towards parents or others, and also make a note as to eagerness of the patient to cooperate.

It is particularly important to keep detailed information as to how the patient, was, is or has been attached to mother, father, and how the separation has been handled, or whether it has been handled at all. Does the patient hate his mother or father? This may determine the transference towards the therapist. Hatred of either parent is a very unfortunate symptom. Notice the dress of the patient and whether it is related in any way to a parent's dress. Are there elements of perfectionism? Is the dress masculine, feminine or neutral? If the patient is a female, is she dominant? If a male, is he passive? Were there any odd, frightening, homosexual experiences, illicit or peculiar sex experiences and traumas? Are there any special fears or anxieties about health, love, marriage, divorce, children, finances or strong insecurities about anything? What is the attitude towards schooling, and at what age did schooling begin and end? How frequently were jobs changed and under what conditions? At what age did the patient stop sleeping in the same room with his mother, father, sister, brother, etc.? Does the patient pay any attention to dreams and what kind of dreams? Are there any special habits like excessive washing, bathing, eating or drinking? Any dislikes of certain foods, unusual fear of dirt? Any nail biting? What are the prohibitions, inhibitions, compulsions

28

or obsessions, if any? What are the special hates? Describe family members who have been neurotic, psychotic or have been in institutions. Are there any family members who have been failures in school, business, or any other undertaking? What have been some of the important successes or failures? Were any of the family members periodic alcoholics, drug addicts, criminals, paupers, very wealthy, or very poor? Any suicides? Were there any religious fanatics or peculiarities in the family?

The above are just a few of the facts which should be elicited from people who enter individual therapy, psychoanalysis or group therapy of any kind, including psychodrama. The more the therapist learns about the patient, student, or subject, through one or more interviews, the better will he know how much, or how far the treatment may be continued and when it might be discontinued. The interviews, if skilfully conducted, should provide the information on which to base at least a tentative diagnosis, and perhaps a prognosis also.

THE CONCEPTS AND STRUCTURE OF PSYCHODRAMA

In the following pages I shall briefly discuss the chief concepts and techniques of the psychodramatic method of psychotherapy. This section constitutes, therefore, a kind of vocabulary of psychodrama, in which the general and basic concepts are presented first, followed by descriptions of specific techniques. Finally, I shall discuss some ideas and related disciplines which, though not exclusive to psychodrama, are nevertheless closely linked to it and may be helpful to an understanding of it.

1) *Tele - Transference - Rapport.* "Tele" is a Greek prefix meaning far-off or distant. We find it in words such as telephone, telepathy, telekinesis, which imply communication or action at a distance. It may also be related to the Greek "telos," a goal, which we find forming part of our word "teleology," which is the study of final causes, or ends, especially as these relate to the concept of design and principle in nature. It is the communication aspect of the word which concerns us here, however. "Tele" is the word used by Moreno to denote the deep insight that occurs in the encounter of one person with another. It is an insight into the "actualities" of another person, whether these actualities are physical, mental, or both. It is the basic bond that lies at the root of all two-way communication. It refers to a bond of perception, a bond of affect, and a bond of love or object relationship. In this sense "transference," the word used by psychoanalysts to describe the particular rapport between therapist and patient, is one aspect of "tele."

30

If the patient or subject was never attached to his father, mother, brother, sister, grandparent, or other relative when he was young, it will be difficult for him to attach himself to the therapist or psychodramatist. He will have a so-called indifferent transference. If he was negative toward one or both of his parents and hated them, he may, in time, hate the therapist. If he had a good object relationship during his youth, his prognosis in psychodrama, group or individual therapy, and psychoanalysis, will probably be good. Therefore, it can be said that the subject's transference on the therapist may be indifferent, positive, or negative, to various degrees. If the original transference was on his parents, then later it could be shifted to the therapist, to various degrees, even to the degree of a transference neurosis. The analyst or therapist may develop a cross transference on the patient or he may be neutral.

If a man and woman had good transferences on their parents, it will be easier for them to transfer on each other, and have a long, lasting love. Otherwise, there may be no love at all, or love for only a short period, or there may develop hostility and difficulties, emotional, neutral, physical and sociological. A good transference upon one's parents is the first step towards happiness, and is the result of good child guidance practices.

If the patient's transference on the therapist is good, it may be easy for the therapist to criticise the patient, in order for him to change. However, if the patient's transference on his therapist is weak, indifferent or negative, then it is dangerous to criticise him, for the patient may hate him, fight or run away, or may talk about the therapist negatively.

It is also possible for a masochistic patient to use any means he can to create troubles and suffering for himself and for the therapist. If the patient learns about his masochism early, and had a former good transference — then the prognosis may be good. Again, if the patient is negative and masochistic, the entire therapeutic pro-

31

cedure is impossible, and the patient may not be acceptable for constructive therapy.

However, the discovery of such facts is sometimes very difficult, and often comes much too late. With a good transference the therapist can take many liberties to criticize, explain and show the patient the real facts in relation to the patient's past, present and future. With a poor or negative transference, the therapist must be extremely cautious and watch his words. It may even be better to halt the therapy. But if that can't be done, then the therapist must never criticize, fight, or frustrate the patient.

The analyst or therapist may play the role not only of therapist but also that of the mother, father, doctor, teacher, authority and religious healer. Some patients may appear over-dependent, and yet be very hostile. The hostility may be open or concealed. If the transference is strong, the over-dependence can be tolerated and handled in due time. In time, independence will be created, together with a positive transference. Many people, including some therapists, fear to accept the role of parents to the patient, and fear to allow the patient to become dependent for a period. The positive transference of a dependent patient can be used to develop his independence, and also for teaching him to accept and like what he should like, and dislike what he should dislike.

When a patient tells the therapist that he looks or acts like the patient's father, it may indicate either a positive or negative transference, depending upon the patient's own relationship to his father. Often the patient may not know whether the transference is positive, negative or indifferent, or whether he is acting out reversal or a reaction formation. For a while the patient could also confuse or fool the therapist.

The patient or subject frequently interprets or reads into the therapist's actions and behavior what may not be the case at all.

32

The patient's interpretations, and sometimes the therapist's, may be correct or incorrect. The patient may complete certain actions or thoughts in his own mind which may not be the therapist's ideas at all. It may be the patient's wishful thinking, or it may be positive resistance, or positive or negative thinking. Many interpretations are wishfulfillments, misunderstandings or resistances. The therapist may occasionally over-interpret or misinterpret; the patient does so frequently. The patient may ascribe to the therapist thoughts and activities which the patient himself is harboring in a positive or negative manner. The patient may be rigid, to the degree that he may not want to change his thoughts and ideas at all, even though the therapist may be very anxious to have the change.

With a good transference the change may come about; with a poor transference, the change may never happen because the neurotic wants to hold on to his neurosis, his masochism, sadism, hostility, (open or disguised) or his negativity.

The transference should be studied, carefully analyzed and understood thoroughly by the therapist and then fully utilized regardless of the criticism that may come. The transference of the patient and the knowledge of the therapist, working together, can bring excellent results, providing there are no complications, no interferences from family members, physicians and teachers, and others who may be jealous, or who may be ignorant of the transference and therapeutic situation. Where there is a good transference and no interference and with regular sessions, the prognosis should be good for the patient.

A combination of psychodrama and other therapeutic methods can hasten results, especially if the therapist does not discount other therapies, but accepts and utilizes all that is involved in transferences, tele, rapport and in gaining insights.

2) *Drama* is the term applied to a poem or other literary material which is written to represent life, history, and the interaction of people, in a form suitable for stage presentation.

Drama is either tragic or comic or a combination of both. At times it may take the form of burlesque, a farce or a melodrama. Both the comedy and the tragedy were originated by the Greeks. The first comedy was performed by Susarian and Dolan on a movable scaffold at Athens in 562 B. C. The first tragedy, performed in 536 B. C. was a drama presented by Thespis, considered as the father of tragedy. Some of the greatest dramatists were Sophocles, Euripides (a tragedian), Aeschylus and Aristophanes (a comedian). In Rome, Plautus, Terence and Seneca were among the great dramatists.

The first English comedy ("Ralph Roister Doister") was written by Nicholas Udall about the middle of the 16th century. However, there is no doubt that the greatest English dramatist of all time was Shakespeare, who was born in 1564 and died in 1616.

A dramatist can either be a writer of a drama or one who acts it out. Generally the term refers to a composer of drama, or a writer of dramatic literature who depicts life emotionalized or exaggerated.

On the psychodramatic stage, the protagonist functions in one or other of two distinct modes, and occasionally in both simultaneously. The first of these modes is the conscious and spontaneous reproduction of scenes from his own past experience, or of material which he has learned from others. In this mode, the protagonist is almost entirely an actor, interpreting factual or emotional realities created outside himself. In the second mode, he functions more as composer, acting out the creations of his unconscious. This mode is very similar to the functioning of the dream process (as hypothesized by psychoanalysis). The dream is unconscious, but is manifested to the director and audience in the manner in which the protagonist acts out situations from his real life.

In both cases the drama lies in the confrontation of the unconscious attitudes and wishes by the objective reality of the situation, which is manifested in the reactions of other persons on the stage to the protagonist's behavior and words. The drama becomes a concrete form of reality-testing. The protagonist literally sees that there may be other ways than his own of reacting to a given situation, and as he tries these out on the stage (at first tentatively, then with growing confidence), he begins to understand his effect on the people around him, and to integrate his new knowledge into behavior that is based on a clearer perception of the realities of any situation. 1302173

3) *Role.* The word "role" is derived from the Latin "Rota," a wheel, and the late Latin word "rotulus," a roll (of parchment). The word "role" was applied by the French first to the roll of paper on which an actor's part was written, and then transferred to the character represented by the actor, with all the traits of personality and modes of thought assigned by the dramatist to this character.

Any society may, in some sense, be thought of as a dramatist, creating roles for the individuals composing that society by the very fact that certain actions or modes of behavior are expected of each individual at different times and places in his life. Everybody has certain ideas of how a mother or a father behaves (or should behave by the standards of society). But the same individual who is a father, in one place and at one time, may also be a judge, a professor, a brother, a bachelor, or even a patient. Society expects the individual to behave differently in some respects towards his father than he would behave towards his brother. Even though certain basic expectations are common to all his roles (kindness, consideration, moral integrity), society has neverthe-

35

less "written" different modes of thought and behavior into the different aspects of his life.

Frequently the disturbance that leads a patient to seek psychodramatic help has arisen from conflict between the expectations of two or more of his roles — a conflict that he is unable to resolve. On the psychodrama stage the individual can act out each of the various roles that make up his total life and personality, and can find new and different ways of interpreting each role. He can act out the roles of other people which impinge on his life, and thereby gain a greater understanding of their feelings toward him, and see how he can adjust his behavior in order to produce feelings and reactions that are more satisfying and rewarding to him than those produced by his current behavior.

4) *Protagonist* is a term applied in psychodrama to the main actor on the stage who tries to dramatize and act out his history, his problems, his personality and his psyche. In this task he is helped by auxiliary egos and the director, usually in the presence of an audience. He first plays his own role, and then the director reverses his role with someone else, who may play the role of a member of his family, a business associate, a teacher, or anyone else.

The protagonist indulges in psychodrama in order that he may act out his feelings on the stage, with his emotions and ideas, so that he can see what has been going on, and also the director, the auxiliary ego, and the audience may witness and feel into the situation. This dramatization usually takes place in a theater especially built for psychotherapy, and this sort of therapy is continued for some time. The protagonist may be a committed patient, a voluntary patient, or a student who comes to the psychodrama stage for training and insights.

36

The protagonist, in time, develops relationships with the director, therapist, auxiliaries and others; these relationships may be of either a positive or a negative nature. There may be positive or negative transferences (tele) which may come and go. Through their interaction, and through the process of role-reversal, the assistants selected by the therapist or the director to help in the drama become, in a sense, extensions of the protagonist himself.

5) *Audience.* One may ask, why is it necessary to have an audience? Strictly speaking, it is not necessary. An effective psychodramatic action can take place with only the protagonist, the director, and one or two auxiliary-egos present. But the audience fulfils a number of important functions which may help to speed up the therapeutic process.

In a spontaneous session where the protagonist has not been previously selected by the director, a member of the audience may quite unexpectedly feel the need to discuss his problem, and he may then become the protagonist of the dramatic action. Then, if someone is needed to play the role of the protagonist's father, or friend, or sibling, the protagonist may choose from the audience a person who in some way resembles this character. He is not restricted to the director's trained assistants; in the audience he may see someone who either physically, or emotionally, or both, gives him the same feeling as the father or friend.

In addition, the members of the audience may identify themselves with the people on the stage, so that they not only understand the subject better, but also understand themselves better, and learn some of the working principles of psychodrama and group psychology. At some future time, members of this audience may be chosen as auxiliaries, and will then be able to function with better understanding of this special process. Then, after the performance, members of the audience can express opinions which can be helpful to all concerned in gaining insights.

Finally after the performance, the director may ask members of the audience how they felt about the procedure and whether they identified positively or negatively with the actors. He may also ask what they thought specifically of the protagonist's actions, his ideas and behavior of the present and past and of his environment. The director may also ask the audience for suggestions. These audience constellations show that some of their members sympathize with real or imaginary characters, or with one or more problems of the subject, or with some collective problems. Sometimes they identify with social problems involving religion, mixed marriages, financial matters, political differences, physical inequalities, or family interference. They may cast light upon various questionable policies which may be rigidly adhered to by the protagonist, his marital partner, or by the protagonist's grandparents and other relatives on one or both sides of the family.

6) *The stage* of the psychodrama consists of a circular platform at three levels, each of which has a special psychological significance. The lowest level, which is one step above the audience floor, may be compared to an individual personality. The second level may be called the visionary level. The third is the action level, where spontaneous action takes place with the realization of various concepts and on various emotional levels.

Sometimes the protagonist cannot be placed on the stage at once, and so he begins at audience floor level. He is gradually advanced to the first step, then to the second, and finally to the third, active stage. We may jump from the floor to the third, or from the first to the third level. The extroverts can reach the top level faster than the introverts. Usually the top level is provided with some chairs, a table, a bed and often a mattress. To the front or back of the stage are several white pillars which support a balcony representing God, authority, father, a leader or some superego personality or qualities.

The *lighting system* and its controls are usually on another balcony towards the back of the stage, and this equipment is controlled by one of the employees, or by a patient who has been in residence for some time. This lighting system (which can be darkened or brightened and also uses different colored lamps), helps to warm up the protagonist, and intensifies moods and emotions so that the protagonist can participate more actively in the psychodrama.

Below, in front, and to the sides of the stage, are a number of members of the audience. If the protagonist or actors object to the presence of certain people in the audience, these may have to be excluded, or else the protagonist may refuse to cooperate, or may block out his role-playing. Sometimes, with the permission of the actors, notes may be taken or there may be a tape recorder in the theater. There have been interesting psychodrama cases when movies have been made. The director and therapist note not only the words, gestures, movements and moods, but also other manifestations of behavior as in postural attitudes, voice placement, facial expressions, tremors, blocking, facial colors, perspiration, anger, fear, worry, indifference, withdrawing, leaning against furniture, kicking, vomiting and running away, and whatever else may come forth from the protagonist and auxiliaries.

7) *Director.* The director seldom takes any role in the psychodramatic action except that of observer and catalyst. He

is invariably a person with experience in psychological and psychodramatic techniques, and must have a high degree of therapeutic insight and understanding. He is usually, therefore, a psychiatrist, a psychologist, or an educator.

The director is the controlling influence in the psychodramatic situation. It is his task, in a spontaneous session, to weld the individuals present into a group, and to ensure that the emotions released are steered into constructive channels. He is a source of information, and guides the action along lines that will produce catharsis and insight for the protagonist and the audience.

It is the director who encourages one or more members of the audience to express some of their feelings about current or past situations in their lives; from these statements he selects those which give a clue to the nature of the individual's problem, and he then encourages that individual to come to the stage and act out certain aspects of the problem. There are specific techniques for encouraging the spontaneity of the patient and getting him into a frame of mind in which he feels safe enough to act out scenes from his life; these techniques are discussed in the section devoted to the warmup.

Once the action has started, the director is constantly on the lookout for clues that will lead naturally and smoothly from one scene into another. But he must also be very aware of all the reactions of the protagonist, and must know how to bypass or avoid situations that are too threatening to the protagonist, and might cause the latter to block or to break off the action.

Although, in the main, it is the protagonist who chooses what aspect of his problem he wishes to explore on the stage, it is the director who has the final power over the action. When he finds that in a certain situation the protagonist is blocking, or evading the real issue by the use of defense mechanisms, the director can force a different reaction from the protagonist by changing the situation; he may bring a new character into the action; he may instruct an assistant to speak aloud the thoughts that are obviously in the protagonist's mind but which he dare not verbalize; or he may instruct the protagonist to watch an assistant repeating the role the protagonist himself has just played so that the latter can see, from outside himself, as it were, what he does and the effect his action has on other people.

The director is the unifying force in the functioning of the entire group, and not least among his tasks is that of inducing the audience, after the action is over, to express their opinions about what went on and to give the protagonist both emotional support and constructive criticism.

8) *Warmup.* Any activity that demands a high degree of effort requires that the participants be allowed a period of time in which to gather their forces for the main effort. It would be unreasonable to rouse an athlete from a deep sleep and immediately dump him on the track, saying, "Run the hundred yards in ten seconds!" Supposing he were capable of doing so, he would still need time to limber up. It would be just as unreasonable to collect a group of people out of their homes, from their dinner, perhaps off the golf course, gather them in a psychodrama theater, put one of them on the stage and immediately tell him, "Say something Significant!" He doesn't know the other people from a hole in the wall, and you expect him to reveal the secrets of his inner life to them? No matter how much he might need the help, he just could not do it.

And so the first part of any psychodrama is spent in welding the individuals into a group, in establishing an emotional tone that is favorable to serious (and perhaps painful) exploration of inner dynamics. Where the individual members of the group already have experience in psychodrama and know each other well, the warmup may be short and consist only in re-establishing a group feeling that has already existed, and in finding a starting point. Such a warmup may take no more than five minutes.

Where the individuals are unknown to each other and have little or no experience of psychodrama, the warmup must be more elaborate. The director is already watching, as the group assembles, to see what constellations form; he notes groups who seem to know each other; he notes any positive or negative interaction that may occur as the people settle in their seats, and also signs that may indicate which individuals are comfortable and relaxed, which are tense and uneasy.

Once the group is seated round the stage, the director will place himself where he can be seen and heard by everyone. If it is a large group he may have to stand on the top level; if the group is small, he will have gathered them close together at the front of the stage, and can establish a more intimate feeling at once by seating himself on the first step. He may ask them to introduce themselves to him and to each other, saying a few words about their occupations and interests, why they have come, and what they expect from the session. During the introductions, the director will be on the lookout for clues that will indicate possible problems, and will be able to pick out one or two individuals who would probably not be afraid to reveal themselves by acting in a scene.

But the director will go cautiously when he attempts to lead such an individual stagewards. The first move will probably be to ask the person to join the director on the first step and just talk a little more. If the group member seems willing (and at this point any momentary uneasiness can be lulled by the director's calm voice and reassuring manner, perhaps reinforced

42

by physical contact—a hand on the shoulder) the director will ease him up to the second step, and then to the action level.

Throughout the warmup period the director explores the group, eliciting from each member some form of participation. If he gets any statement from one person that indicates a particular attitude, he may ask other members of the audience whether they agree. He may throw out some statement that is bound to elicit an opposite reaction from some member of the audience. In short, by every means at his disposal from charm of manner to subtle prodding, he will use this initial period to get as many members of the audience as possible to express ideas and feelings, and to function as a group. Only when this feeling tone has been established will any individual feel safe to reveal parts of his life.

9) *Auxiliary Ego.* The auxiliary egos are the characters with whom the protagonist interacts on the stage. They represent those facets of people in the protagonist's environment which directly impinge on the protagonist. Such characters are seldom seen "in the round," since the facets of their personality which do not impinge on the protagonist have little significance; they are seen by director and audience through the eyes of the protagonist himself. Individuals who are chosen as auxiliary egos must be alert to clues from the protagonist which will enable them to reproduce the emotional effect of the originals. Sometimes the individuals playing auxiliary egos have difficulty in catching the right emotional tone in which to play their part; this is a case where role-reversal is of the utmost value. The auxiliary ego temporarily takes over the role of the protagonist, while the protagonist himself plays the role of the parent, sibling, lover, or other character in question, and *shows* the director, auxiliary ego, and audience how the original individual would have behaved (or actually did behave) in the scene being played

43

out. When the protagonist has portrayed the right emotional tone of the scene, the roles are reversed once more — the protagonist reverts to his own role, and the auxiliary ego to that of the parent, sibling or lover, armed with the knowledge that will enable him to react realistically to the protagonist.

The auxiliary ego functions mainly on a conscious level; in his role he is mainly concerned with *reproducing* responses — either the responses that the original character actually did give, or the responses that the protagonist would have liked him to give. But the auxiliary ego inevitably functions to some extent on an unconscious level also, because of his own personality makeup. He may find himself in conflict during a scene, because the type of response required of him is either contrary to his nature, or because the situation triggers reactions in him that operate on an unconscious level and are intimately linked to his own problems. Thus, in attempting to act in a certain way in order to help the protagonist, he may receive insight into the reasons for his own difficulties.

10) *Soliloquy.* This word derives from the Latin words "solus," alone, and "loqui," to speak. It is usually applied to the act of speaking aloud one's thoughts and ideas, without addressing any other person. The speaker is, in fact, talking to himself.

There is a considerable difference between a soliloquy and a monologue. A monologue is a speech, of considerable length, uttered by one person, in the presence of others and for their consideration. The difference lies in the *intention* rather than in the fact of others being present. Browning's dramatic monologues, for example, were written to be spoken by a single person, but with the clear intention of conveying information and ideas to the audience. Hamlet's famous soliloquy ("To be or not to be, that is the question . . .") was not only spoken when he was alone, but is clearly not intended to be heard by anyone else. Hamlet is, so to say, using himself as a sounding-board; he is in conflict, and speaks aloud his thoughts in the hope that as he hears them spoken the ideas will become clearer and he will be able to resolve the conflict one way or another. A prayer spoken to God is another form of soliloquy.

The soliloquy is extremely meaningful in psychodrama. Frequently, after a scene in which the protagonist has experienced powerful emotions which he has not clearly identified or is reluctant to acknowledge, the director will isolate the protagonist on the stage and encourage him to try to verbalize his feelings in soliloquy. The isolation is usually accomplished by having the protagonist sit with his back to the audience and by dimming the lights, so that a psychological space is inserted between the protagonist and his immediate surroundings.

Under these conditions he is able to verbalize feelings and thoughts of a kind not ordinarily expressed in public. If he has difficulty in verbalizing, an auxiliary ego may sit beside him and speak some of these words for him. Often a soliloquy becomes a dialogue between two conflicting aspects of the protagonist's personality; he may speak both parts, or he may speak one part while the auxiliary ego verbalizes the other part. When acting in one of the protagonist's roles, the auxiliary ego is said to be his "double."

11) Ordinarily, the *double* in psychodrama is not a double or a dual personality. A double is an auxiliary who acts as an extension of the protagonist. He may also try to make a second personality out of the protagonist, in order to help the protagonist to understand himself better by emoting more, exaggerating, questioning, belittling, doubting, saying the opposite or repeating for emphasis the words of the protagonist.

45

If the protagonist says: "I am going home tomorrow," the double may say: "Am I really going home tomorrow?" "Is it best for me to go home tomorrow?" Or he may say: "Oh, yes, I had better go home tomorrow because I am needed at home. I will save some money. I may be able to go to school, get a job, etc." Or the double may say: "Yes, my parents want me to go home, or my wife and children need me at home. I will decide for myself. Should I waste time here or am I really getting somewhere? If I am getting somewhere, what have I learned?" Or, "The hell I am going home!"

The protagonist may be unable to say these things himself, so that the double helps to stimulate him with these additional remarks and thoughts. Since the double is an extension of the protagonist, he is part of him. These two people, or when there are still more auxiliaries, all together, make up one person and act out as one person. Then other individuals may personify the father, mother, husband, wife, child, employer, teachers, neighbor, etc.

The protagonist may demonstrate autistic thinking by illustrating wishes and desires which are not realistic, or which may fantasize imaginary gratifications or longings, or may fantasize life through poetry, dreams, or paranoid states, as in dereistic thinking. The double or auxiliary may exaggerate these thoughts to make the protagonist laugh at himself or ask: "Am I dreaming? Am I going crazy? Do I really believe these thoughts, or am I making them up? Maybe I really do not believe these things. I am only trying to make an impression to fool people, to get sympathy, or to punish myself and others. Maybe I'm only trying to confuse myself or to act ridiculously, so that I will not have to work, go to school, or pay my debts. Am I trying to exhibit myself, so that I can say just anything and not be afraid to do so? Is my mental state influenced by delusions, so that my imaginary life takes the leading role in my

46

behavior? Am I eclectic, whereby I organize into a comprehensive system, with compatible factors drawn from otherwise incompatible theories and experiences, or am I syncretic, where I combine incompatible systems uncritically? Maybe I talk and act without a definite goal, hoping that by brain-storming myself, something may come out which may be of help to me or to someone else. Perhaps if I talk a lot with gestures, I may develop a strong degree of feeling and then I will be able to exhibit myself to others, or to myself, for some kind of self-improvement. Maybe the doctor will think more of me."

Much of this spontaneous acting on the psychodrama stage is phenomenological. Many of the actions, emotions and thoughts are subliminal, ineffective or useless. Some of the behavior may be useful or insightful.

The double can make the protagonist's statements and actions more forceful; he can repeat some of the protagonist's statements and actions in order to intensify their ambivalence and ambiguity; he can give a double interpretation or soliloquize for the protagonist.

The double may also become hypercritical, deceitful, or insincere, in order to stir up the protagonist. The double may exaggerate, intensify or minimize certain emotions or aims of the protagonist. The double should know psychology and psychiatry and human relations. At times he may act as the protagonist's unconscious. He may duplicate or counter some of the protagonist's statements. He may also be ready to take the protagonist's place, should the protagonist cease talking or acting and block out temporarily. The double may cast doubt on the protagonist's statements or actions, whether these be right or wrong. Or he may just duplicate the behavior of the protagonist.

The double must either be a good psychologist or have great

47

intuition, or both. He should also have the ability to act with and against the protagonist.

The double may help the protagonist to emotionalize either by supporting him, or by prodding and antagonizing him. The double may also express himself in terms of a double meaning, making the protagonist think of indelicate or questionable matters, to which the protagonist has made veiled reference but which he is afraid to speak of openly. The double may express a double meaning whether decent or indecent, as in the English grammatical form, the so-called double-entendre which was much used by Dryden and his contemporaries.

Doubles in English can be something like: "love of labor or labor of love," "his reference, reference of his," "one's food is another's poison," "the money of the rich is the blood of the poor," etc. These may be double genitives or possessives. "The cat's paw or the paw of the cat." This multiple meaning may be the cat's own paw, or the paw of a mouse which the cat was eating, or a reference to the monkey who pulled the chestnuts out of the fire with the cat's paw so as not to burn his own — this cat was perhaps the first patsy!

The doubles may use the expression of double negatives, such as: "It would not shock me if he would not pay his debts."

Sometimes the double can use double-talk for the purpose of confusing or exciting the protagonist, and so getting him more involved instead of intellectualizing. There are very many techniques for the double to use in accomplishing his aim of freeing the protagonist to express freely all his emotions, of whatever kind. The double should pick these techniques according to the needs of the moment, the instructions of the director, and the double's own experience and ability to use these techniques.

48

12) *Ego, Ego-Ideal, Alter-Ego, and Altruism.* Since many people are confused about the meaning of the term Ego, perhaps this term should be clarified. The average person may think of the ego as being the individual's conception of himself and his personality reactions. The word often has connotations of a person who is aggressive, independent, over self-confident, and has strong wishes to get what he wants.

"Ego" is the Latin word for "I," and pertains to individuality and personality.

Freud explained the ego as that part of the unconscious which breaks off from the Id into consciousness, and that part of the mind which is modified by the external world through the senses. It is energy which is related to consciousness.

Much has been said about the ego, because it is an important term. Much of ego psychology revolves around the term ego. However, it was introduced from the Latin into philosophy by the great Descartes; it was then borrowed by Freud, who extended its meaning and values and also derived other psychoanalytical terms from it.

The philosophers used ego extensively to denote the conscious self, or a person whose activity is supposed to come from the world of experience. The psychoanalysts enlarged upon ego, claiming that it was developed and sprung from the id. The id, as it grew up from infancy in the world of experience, finally became conscious. Then the ego and consciousness coincided in many respects.

The ego's first function is to test reality and to act as a go-between between the id and superego, by selection and control of the demands of the id and the superego. It functions as a governor between the id and the superego.

At times the word ego-hood may help to explain ego, when

it pertains to a situation where we must face or avoid a reality, but the reality is that of the individual himself, and it pertains more to the "I."

An egoist is self opinionated and is obsessed with operations and ideas of his own mind. He repeats to excess the word "I," and talks too much about himself and magnifies his own achievements and power.

From ego, we also have *alter-ego,* which is an individual's conception of another being. He differentiates his wants from the wants of others.

Ego alter or alter-ego is a functional construct which hypothesizes that the origin of social organization or institution is a combination of the energies of egoism and altruism. Here there are self-narcissistic interests, together with drives for self preservation and race preservation. Theoretically, social interaction includes the developed ego which develops further into the alter superego and which functions in the exact opposite of id-narcissitic influences.

Alter-ego is another self which can also be an auxiliary ego or a double. A similar expression, alter egoism, comes from the Latin, "alter-ego" or a second or other "I," which means an altruistic feeling or sympathy for others who are in a similar situation. The empathy may be between the protagonist and the director and vice versa, or between the auxiliary ego and the protagonist (I love or hate me) or others.

The alter-ego may be similar to *ego ideal* which may cause a person to work less for himself and more for others, to avoid being censured by his moral conscience. The ego ideal will not permit him to remain with his childish ego which in the past, he found self sufficient. He gradually finds satisfaction in helping others, in addition to helping himself.

There is a great deal of distance between ego ideal and the real ego, but in an immature individual the ego ideal does not lie too far from the ego, and his emotions are childish. A mature person develops mutual and altruistic relations between the ego and the object, which may be the marital partner, parent, sibling, or members of the community. He develops empathy with other people, and he is not fixated on his own personal selfishness.

Ego ideal is a psychoanalytic term meaning what youngsters aim at — perfection, by recognizing and identifying themselves with persons whom they love or admire. These characters may come from the family group, outsiders, or even literary characters. The characters of the ego ideal may be great gangsters, athletes, politicians, warriors, artists, religious figures, teachers, family members, scientists, or others. In the very young, the identifications may be with policemen, firemen, cowboys, etc. Later on the ego ideals are people with more mature values. One or more of these identified characters may influence the protagonist's behavior on the stage and also his attitudes may be swayed by such images.

Usually the ego ideal is made up of a number of characters — all fused into one personality with their character traits and attitudes in the background. In most cases, the first identification and ego ideal comes from the mother or father, or both, and other members of the family; then come teachers, religious characters, movies, TV and athletic figures.

Some individuals develop ego ideals from two types of values: They accept the dualistic theory in action, assuming that the psychic and physical phenomena are both real, but differ in nature, so that they accept some values from great physical characters and other values from individuals with great mental accomplishments.

Usually, the higher the development of the individual the

better are his values, which were based on ego ideals gotten from great men and women; hence, he places more importance on mental than on physical achievements. Those with lower intelligence and education may place greater value on prize fighters, baseball heroes and football stars.

Another ego, the *superego,* is the offspring of the id and the ego. It is worthwhile to think of the ego as being a deciding element in controlling impulses, tendencies and inspirations which come both from id and from superego — the ego resolves conflicts between the id and the superego.

With a poorly developed superego and with poor ego ideals, there must co-exist a neurosis and excessive self-love, manifested in a poor relationship between ego and object.

Altruism is a word used in religion, psychology, philosophy, ethics and sociology. It was coined by Auguste Comte who lived in the early part of the 19th century. He claimed that the chief reason for existence was to live for the sake of others. Altruism refers to a person's disposition and conduct toward the well being of others. It is the exact opposite of egoism which denotes a self centered character. One is for the good of others; the other is mostly for the good of the self. Frequently, altruism, morality and ethics are closely related.

According to Freud, the child is completely egotistical and narcissistic, and wants what he wants. It is only later in life that he develops morals and altruism. The maternal instinct is not necessarily altruistic or egoistic. The conscious direction of the self is usually developed as the child comes to differentiate between the self and the not-self (alter); thus, a conscious pursuit for the interest of others or self is developed. Altruistic and ethical theory, which includes morality, is an important development in the child's maturation.

In psychodrama there is considerable talk about ego, auxiliary-ego and alter-ego, where the protagonist is often narcissistic at the beginning, but later becomes somewhat altruistic by seeing the side of the other fellow, when he reverses his role and sees himself acting out together with others, who are involved in the psychodrama.

An ego-altruist is a person whose sentiments are such that he wants self-gratification, but also wants gratification in others. The ego-altruist boosts himself and others. He is almost the opposite of the ego narcissist.

Superego is part of ego psychology. It is part of a functional construct consisting of a mental apparatus which criticizes the ego and often causes anxieties and punishment if the ego tends to become over influenced by the id. It is an unconscious conscience, and functions as a reaction-formation to the id. The superego may have symbolic factors which may not be comprehended by the actor.

13) *Symbology.* The actor's ideas, gestures or emotions, may represent a substitute for other ideas of past experiences. Here the psychiatrist or psychologist may recognize symbolization and explain to the protagonist, in private or in the group, the working of symbolization as it occurs in dreams, fantasies, myths, puns, satire and neurotic manifestations. The symbols may be condensations or indirect assumptions expressed in figurative forms. At times the actors are syncretic, when they poke fun at the director (perhaps mistaken for a parent), or at other members on or off the stage, parent substitutes and other figures. Often this is a type of childish thinking and getting satisfaction by sort of unconscious and conscious behavior combined. Frequently little children play such games, in which they connect everything with everything, though not in conscious, realistic or adult conceptions.

The actors on the psychodrama stage may be realistic or unrealistic, or a combination of the two. They may play music, dance, sing, box, fight, perform acrobatics, even perform transvestism either for poking fun or for negative reasons. The psychodrama stage demands no special kind of clothing but the type of clothing chosen may have symbolic meaning.

Occasionally the protagonist or auxiliaries are zoophiliacs, which means they love animals to excess. Under such conditions they may personify a dog or a cat, or use an animal to represent themselves or others. They may symbolize a man through an animal, or use an animal as a symbol representing a trait or an idea.

The protagonist may also, in the case of megalomania (where they over-evaluate themselves), use a pig, mouse, or bug to symbolize a parent, an authoritative individual, a doctor, teacher, or an idea. This is an attempt by the protagonist to show how much better he is than others, with whom he expects to contend.

Some actors make deliberate errors to get attention, castigate those in the theatre, poke fun, or use the errors against their having been belittled or laughed at for past errors.

As to insights to be gotten from psychodrama, the perception comes from both conscious performance on the stage, and from understanding of the unconscious symbolic terms and symbolic gestures. Perception does not necessarily come from sensory attributes.

We may gain perception suddenly or we may know the analytical component, and relative condition, and then work backwards for the purpose of reconstructing the perception out of empirical elements. Hence, perception may come from genetics, and may not necessarily be chronological in nature. It must be remembered that we do not usually derive perception from assembling sensory attributes. More often we gain perception from an analysis of past events, plus synthesizing. Hence, a perception is a complete experiential entity, and is not, within itself, a composite of similar experiences. But it is a reflection in experience of a similar physiological condition, which is a projection into the sensorium of events, in the phenomenal world.

These thoughts can be concluded from Gestalt psychology. Memory color can be perceived repeatedly without actually repeatedly seeing the color. Also, size constancy of objects may retain magnitude regardless of distance. The famous figure-ground relationship of objects and forms have given peculiar perception with visual illusion of size, shape and direction. Gestalt psychology has greatly influenced our understanding through the special divisions of psychology into the terms of visual and audile perception, which gives us the prototype of all mental structure, form and organization.

The other sensory perceptions, Gestalts, have not as yet been as far developed as the perceptions of seeing and hearing, and principally the perceptions of distance, color, space, form, direction, aesthetics and illusions. Perception, memory, symbolism and semantics, are most important for insights, understanding and interpretation of people's actions. The therapist must be, above all, *a good psychologist.*

14) *Catharsis.* Historically, catharsis was first defined by Aristotle in his "Poetic" when he noticed the peculiar affects of the Greek drama upon the spectators. He thought that drama was one of the means of purifying the spectators, through excitation of the emotions, which would relieve, in part at least, their selfish passions. He could have added that it could relieve, in part, some tensions and anxieties, as well.

Moreno leans heavily on catharsis, but has displaced the emphasis of the affect from the spectators onto the actors. Moreno believes that catharsis and spontaneity in psychodrama are two valuable forces which create healing effects on the actors, probably by relieving tensions and anxieties, and giving the actors a better understanding of themselves; hence, they learn to exercise better control.

Moreno believes that protagonist and auxiliaries are more or less forced, by their own will, to act out and show spontaneous behavior, which may be abreacted cathartically while depicting their actual living and their home life on a stage before and through a group; thus, both the actors themselves and the audience can identify and participate emotionally in the various roles, and see the various sides of the actor's life, and the environments, both actually and symbolically. It appears that the actor experiences both passive and active catharsis through this psychodramatic process on the live stage, causing the spectators and the actors to identify themselves as one person. Here we have a relationship between a number of people working for and against each other, and finally, through the role-playing, finding a common road toward reality. Through the role-playing and catharsis, the actors finally find themselves in their sociometry, and can place themselves where they and other members of their family belong, or should belong. They may learn why and how they have been rejected, neglected, spoiled, or chosen; where they were given too much recognition, were disliked, or were placed in the proper position; and where they should belong in relationship to others.

Catharsis, on the other hand, although used in psychodrama, is more germane to psychoanalytic method, because patients have a charge of energy which is invested in an idea, with feeling and significance, and which may pertain to one or more people — most often the father, mother and sister — expressed in anxieties or other emotions, when there are associations to these people, or with whom they are identified. Under such conditions, there may be mental tensions unexplainable otherwise.

15) *Sociometry.* Sociometry is a hybrid word formed from the Latin "socious," meaning a fellow or companion, and the Greek "metria," meaning the action of measuring. Sociometry denotes the art of measuring the social forces acting upon a group of people. These forces may tend either to knit the group closely together or to disperse it; the effects of these forces are particularly manifested in the attractions and repulsions existing between individual members of the group. Moreno and his co-workers have evolved effective means of measuring the existence and relative strength of these forces.

Through sociometry, as a result of experience and analysis, we may discern the laws and tendencies shown by the psychological situations existing in a community. These patterns may be used to prognosticate the behavior of a group or one of its members. Sociologists, notably Gibson and Hebb in 1949, have pointed out that social responses are determined by something else or in addition to the immediately preceding sensory stimulation.

Morgan, Beach and Kleitman expounded upon a central theme to the effect that there is a central excitatory mechanism and an interest, which is a set pattern of behavior or attitudes which will cause a group to react in a manner in which response is independent to a great degree of a present stimulus, but may be excited by a past attitude or may be triggered as a response to the suggestion of a leader who may be partially right or wrong. This reaction is similar to a mob psychological reaction, stirred up mostly by one person. Such a reaction is both unreasonable and full of emotion and is therefore unpredictable.

These concepts describe a relatively autonomous component of behavior, which is in some way conceived as an interval of the organism, yet it has a degree of autonomy from external stimulation, which plays more or less a central determining role in behavior. These patterns seek meaning and strive in some way after a "fit."

This social scheme connotes a *preparatory activity* which may be called by the term "set"; it may, at times, be less active, but is ready to perform according to a certain pattern or scheme. This scheme is more or less a sharpening of attitudes and behavior is in a definite set direction. This scheme may "fractionate" in part, or to great degree, may influence an individual's role.

Sociogram is from the French "socio" and the Latin "socious," meaning companion, helper or associate, plus gram. Engram comes from the German "enen" plus grammar, meaning a picture, a form, a letter, a trace or something drawn.

Psychologically, all experiences leave behind in the brain traces which may be conscious or unconscious. Our memory system is based upon memory traces.

16) *Sociogram* is the diagrammatic result of a sociometric test performed on a population. A sociogram shows the patterns of the relationship existing between the individuals in a group which has been tested. The sociogram makes possible a description of the condition and attitude of the behavior of every individual, with reference to the combined feelings and behavior of all the people in the particular area. It explains individual attitudes and behavior in that particular society which could not have been revealed by the ordinary methods. Here we see the emotional attraction of certain people and their rejection of others, both in small and large groups. We see individuals being repulsed by leaders in the group or by certain cliques.

This sociogram results from sociometric tests which reveal the underlying attraction-repulsion pattern of a group, which may not be manifested without the test, and it reveals little cliques and bigger cliques in a society. Sometimes you may also get right and wrong reasons for social attractions and repulsions. Often these reasons may be prejudiced, hostile, erroneous, ignorant or exaggerated.

The sociometric test is an instrument which measures the mind of an organization as shown in one or more social groups. The basic instrument is an individual's choice of associates in any group which he would like to join as a member. This test shows clearly that the underlying attraction-repulsion pattern of a group differs widely from what is visible on the surface. Such tests have been applied to small and large groups, schools, religions, home groups and working groups. This same test can also be applied to groups and individuals who would choose psychopathic or criminal groups in preference to other groups. These choices may come from forgotten memory traces in the unconscious and from positive and negative transferences or tele. Most of the real causes may have been forgotten or may have originated from prejudices, ignorance and misinformation or from rumor and propaganda. Mob action could be similar to sociopathic and psychopathic behavior.

A *sociopath* is really a psychopath. It is synonymous with psychopathic personality.

Sociopathology is a term applied to the pathology of society. There are individuals in a group who are psychopaths and who influence society, or one society is more inclined to pathology than another.

Social-mobility is a word used to mean that there are free exchanges and free interaction between people or groups and

59

they can also more or less freely change roles. It is the opposite of social rigidity.

Social mores stands for the meaning of roles or codes which people assume — whether they accept unwritten moral standings upon one or more people in a group — which influence the social behavior in a society or culture. These unwritten laws vary in time, geography and culture.

A *social factor* is an individual who influences one or more people in his group or groups. He may also be called an instigator for good or bad. The auxiliary egos, may act as social factors upon the protagonist, director, audience, etc.

A *social neuter* is different from a social activator or instigator. He, more or less, has no effect upon the behavior of his group or other groups because of his indifference or weakness. The protagonist may or may not be a social neuter on the director, audience, etc.

Social fixity. By these two words, it is believed that one or more people can be so fixed in their social communication and behavior that their roles are rigid, and their status remains stationary. Some people on the psychodrama stage behave in a fixed manner while others may become mobile.

Social hunger is a wish to be accepted by a club, organization, community or a special group. Individuals crave social favor and fear social disapproval. Many join clubs and organizations for fear of being left out or being alone. Often individuals will spend fortunes of money for social acceptance, or will not give to charity, but spend years of studying, and force themselves through college, even though it may appear impractical to their realities. Many people restrict their inclinations and behavior because of fear of social disapproval. In group therapy where one's defenses are still operating properly, he would certainly prefer social approval. Perhaps while interacting on the stage, he may not do what he wants, but what he thinks the group wants, in order to meet with their approval and, in this way, get altruistic thoughts, thereby minimising his egotism, narcissism and, perhaps lessen his neurotic and infantile thoughts. The protagonist may be blessed with social hunger and therefore, try harder for social approval and hence, talk, act and be more spontaneous.

17) *Sociodrama.* Sociodrama can be considered a part of sociometry. Sociodrama is more concerned with collective problems; therefore, it is often different from the psychodrama activities on the stage, because in psychodrama there is usually a subject with a main single problem, and possibly with some minor smaller problems. But in sociodrama the main issues are of a collective nature, and the actors, assume general roles experienced in a collective manner, which must be portrayed collectively.

In psychodrama the director is more concerned with the individual, whereas in sociodrama the director is more concerned with the group. However, in both, roles are played by more than one actor. The roles in psychodrama are more or less confined to one individual at a time whereas the roles in sociodrama represent collective thoughts and past experiences of fathers, mothers and others, which include more than one problem at a time. For example, in psychodrama there is deep action method dealing with inter-personal relations involving mostly private and individual philosophies resulting from the influences of others. In sociodrama the same deep action method deals with inter-group relations which may include not only individual ideas but also racial, religious, political and similar collective philosophies, on top of individual inter-personal relations. Very often it is very difficult to separate these two types of action, for usually one includes or influences the other. But the role playing in psychodrama stresses the individual inter-relations whereas in sociodrama, the stress is upon group and complex ideas, which go along with the inter-personal relations.

In psychodrama the stress may deal with behavior, action, and ideas relating to my personal problems with my mother and my father, or with positive or negative emotions and attitudes relating to them. In sociodrama, the stress may relate to my ideas and fixations upon a definite political party view, or some religious views, or national attachments, which frequently dominate my attitude and behavior. Very frequently, both psychodrama and sociodrama are involved in the same person, who will perform upon the stage simultaneously exemplifying the results of psychodrama and sociodrama.

18) *Sociatry.* "Sociatry" is a word coined by Dr. J. L. Moreno, and is analogous to the word "psychiatry." Psychiatry, though it takes account of normal functioning of the human mind, is more specifically concerned with the abnormal and pathological in the mental makeup of the individual. Likewise, sociatry, while it must of necessity understand and recognize normal patterns of behavior of a society, is primarily concerned with the abnormal — that is, with what one might call social pathology. In sociatry, the abnormal patterns under observation are manifested in deviant behavior either of a whole group in relation to other groups, or of an individual with specific reference to his social function within a group.

Psychodrama is one of the instruments most useful in sociatry, since it inherently entails group functioning, and reveals not only the reaction of an individual within a group in certain situations, but also the couter-reaction of the whole group to the subsequent behavior of the individual.

SUMMARY AND CONCLUSIONS

From what has been said, it is clear that psychodrama is a form of depth therapy that combines action methods with group psychotherapy and socioanalysis. It involves one individual (the protagonist) upon whose problem the attention is mainly focused, in interaction with a group of persons. The problems are explored by means of dramatic methods which involve a number of people of the group, and since many of these are liable to have problems which are closely related to those of the protagonist, catharsis and insight is by no means limited to any one group member.

Both the protagonist and the audience begin to find that they have many problems in common, and to understand the origin and effect of these problems. They also explore together various methods of achieving solutions to the problems. There is a forced identification between members of the audience and the protagonist or his extensions on the stage, which brings about an enhanced level of communication between every person present.

The psychodramatic stage, then, is an extension of the world, both within and beyond reality, and provides a means of exploring both real facts and also phantasies and unrealistic situations. When the protagonist attempts to portray his private world and his perception of the people around him, he does so in actions as well as in words; these actions help to free his expression of his emotions, and the more often he acts out his real self on the stage, the more spontaneous and involved he becomes.

It should be noted that the safety and freedom of the environment encourages honest expression of feelings that are normally concealed from a world in which expression of such feelings has previously resulted in highly threatening consequences or reactions. Role playing is by no means a new experience to any person who attends a psychodrama session — each of these individuals has been playing many roles ever since his infancy. The difference lies in the fact that the individual has hitherto been unaware that he has been playing roles in the real world, and that it is in the nature of these roles to change at different times in his life. Nor does he realize, indeed, that it is the sum of all these roles that makes up the self, not the self that creates the roles.

It is, therefore, not merely role-playing which opens our eyes, but to an even greater degree the opportunity of role-change and role-reversal in a given situation, while this situation is being acted out in a safe environment from which no hurtful consequences can attend such experimentation. The psychodramatic stage, therefore, offers the possibility of an enormous enlargement in the range of the roles an individual can play, and so can bring about deep insight into the efficiency and appropriateness of the roles he actually does play in the real world. Of course, it is a great deal easier for people who know each other well to exchange roles, than for people between whom there is a wide social or intellectual distance. But here again, the opportunity for free experimentation and continued practice in role-exchange permits each individual to acquire a far greater and more intimate knowledge of other people than he ever had before.

It is easily observable that every person present at a psychodrama session becomes involved, to a greater or lesser extent, in the action that takes place on the stage. Indeed, everyone present functions, at least partially, in the role of therapist. Their observations can help the protagonist to obtain insight into his behavior and attitudes; but at the same time the auxiliaries and the audience are also subject to forced identification and to a high degree of insight into their own behavior and attitudes. It would probably also be true to say that the more open the auxiliaries and audience are to such insights, the more help they can give the protagonist. Hence we can conclude that patients may in time become classed as adjunct therapists.

Any individual can, in a few sessions and with a few explanations, learn the principles underlying the roles of protagonist, auxiliary ego, and double, so that he can carry out role-reversal and mirror activities when called upon by the director to do so. But it may take quite a number of sessions over quite a long period before he has attained sufficient insight into his own behavior and motivations to enable him to function at maximum efficiency in these roles. As a protagonist, complete involvement in the action is called for; the protagonist will derive little benefit from playing out scenes on a purely intellectual level. If he remains intellectual, he merely repeats the defenses that he puts up against the real world; only when he can spontaneously act and express his true emotions does he expose his real self in a manner that will permit him to be helped.

From the director and auxiliaries, on the contrary, a considerable degree of detachment is demanded. If they are to be effective in helping the protagonist to encounter himself and re-integrate himself personally and sociologically, they cannot afford to become involved to the point where their own emotional reactions to a situation could color their perception of the protagonist's reactions. They must, in fact, put aside their own emotions except in so far as these can be channeled into the service of the protagonist. Yet in another sense the director and auxiliaries are constantly treading the fine dividing line between the degree of emotionality that would obscure their perceptions and the degree of detachment that would alienate the protagonist. There must always be kindness, understanding, patience, and the non-judgmental acceptance of facts that is proper to a scientist who is trying to learn in order to be of help.

It is difficult to determine how far, and in what way, the psychodramatic form of therapy is preferable to other forms. Much depends upon the personality makeup of the patients, their normal environment, their finances, and what they and their families have previously heard about therapy of any sort. But it is probably safe to say that patients who are not strongly psychotic, who have some intellectual background, and who are attracted to this method, will do well regardless of whether they work in an amorphous, unstructured group or in a highly organized group. Probably the most fruitful line of approach would be to place such patients in an amorphous group until they are acclimated to the method, and then to transfer them to a structured group in which attention can be focused on specific problems the moment they are strong enough to explore these. Conversely, a patient who is making little progress in a structured group could be transferred to an amorphous group for a while. But to attain the maximum benefits from the method, each and every patient should function as often as possible both as auxiliary and as protagonist — and perhaps even attempt the direction of a session under the guidance of the regular director.

As a final word, it should be remembered that psychodrama is a most flexible and potent tool. Though a special stage and the presence of an audience are therapeutically desirable for maximum effect, they are not necessary. The only basic elements of the method are role-playing, role-change, and role-reversal, and with the help of a director and one or two auxiliaries these can be carried out almost anywhere. Nor is the method's usefulness restricted to the treatment of abnormal or deviant behavior; it can be used effectively with normal people to help them solve even the most ordinary and common problems of being human. With only minor adaptations it can be used in the emotional education of children. And the understanding of oneself and of others that results from the experience of psychodrama can be of inestimable benefit to any and every individual. But *experience* is the keyword here — though reading and study can be helpful in leading an individual to an understanding of the rationale behind psychodrama, it is only through personal experience with it that he will be able to put such knowledge to practical and effective use in his own life.

A PSYCHODRAMA SESSION IN ACTION

D — stands for Director
P — Protagonist
AX — Auxiliary Ego
Db — Double
M — Mother
F — Father
S — Sister
GF — Grandfather
GM — Grandmother
A — Audience

D — Ladies and Gentlemen, tonight we shall have a psychodrama with P as the protagonist. I would first like to introduce some of the people present tonight so that we will know a little about each other. Then we shall choose the dramatic staff for the stage. I see we have in our audience Dr. X, who is professor of Sociology at Columbia, and his lovely wife. Please stand up, Dr. X. (Audience applauds.) I also see we have here Professor Y, who is on the faculty of Wagner College. (Applause.) Where is your lovely wife?

Y — She's visiting with some friends who are ill.

D — I also see Mrs. Z. Mrs. Z is a social worker with the Department of Public Welfare. She has attended many of our sessions and is a friend of the psychodrama stage. She has had experience in acting some years back. (As she stands, there is applause.) This young man with the red bow tie, please stand and introduce yourself. (He stands and says, "I am a junior student at City College, majoring in psychology with a minor in sociology.")

D — You are welcome here and we hope you will enjoy it. Miss B in the far corner, will you please introduce yourself.

Miss B — I am Miss B, a student at Vassar College. I am here tonight with my mother because we are interested in psychodrama.

D — You are certainly welcome and we hope that you can come again. Now, as you know, or will find out, psychodrama is the method or technique of acting out on the stage of one or more problems involving history, psychology, sociology, music, or what have you, in a group fashion so that one or more people can show themselves and others what has been in their past and what is happening at the present. The purpose is to learn what the group thinks is the real problem, to see how it came about, and also to offer some possible solutions or suggestions. After one or more sessions, one or more solutions may be suggested or achieved by the protagonist himself, by the rest of the people, or by all together, in combination. There is a considerable body of literature in this field, which you can find in large libraries. I would suggest that you all do some reading up on psychodrama, so that you will understand better this kind of approach as therapy.

It will be easier for us to cooperate if you participate in a psychodrama. But read some of the literature before such participation. (Pause.) Now, is there someone who has a problem and who would like to submit it to psychodrama? (Mr. P raises his hand.)

D — Come forward and stand beside me. Please give us your name and a little background or history on yourself. Then try to state one or two problems which you think could be aired out in this session.

P — My name is P. I live with my mother and father in New Jersey. Oh, yes, I also have a sister. My grandfather and grandmother live in the same town and visit us once every two or three weeks. I am finishing high school this June and want to attend an out of town college. My father demands that I go to school in New York City, which is near our home. I would like to go to school a great distance away from home, but within the United States.

D — All right, take a chair on the stage. Who in the audience would you prefer to act with you on the stage? Please choose your father, mother, sister and grandparents.

P — (Pointing.) I would like these five people to represent my family.

D — Very well, will these five people take seats on the stage? (To P.) Where does your family usually congregate to talk? Describe it.

P — This is the living room. A couch is against that wall, with a table next to it. Across the room is a little table with a TV set on it. There are book shelves against the other wall and a window on this side and one at

70

the other side. The floor is covered with carpets and the walls are painted green, with a white ceiling. We have a floor lamp here and a ceiling lamp at the other side. When my father is not home our dog and cat may also be here, but when he is home these animals are either in the garage or in the yard.

D — Very well, you are now talking to your father and mother about your future schooling.

P — (To F.) Dad, you know that it is high time that I make a choice for college. You know that I don't want to go to a school too close to home. I want to go to school out west, like Wisconsin or California, or else to one in the South, like Tulane, Georgia or Florida. Or perhaps up north to Cornell.

F — Now look, Son, you know how I feel about it. You are going to attend a college in New York City and nothing else. I will pay for it and you will do as I say, or else you will go to work and forget about college.

M — But dear, you shouldn't be so strict and rigid with your ideas. Let's think about this. Suppose he won't study if he attends a city college? What good will that do?

F — I ask you, do you want to pay for his college education?

S — Dad, I think Mother is right. Why must you be so rigid and authoritarian?

F — You get the hell out of here! This is not your business.

P — You don't have to get so emotional. Look what you

have done to Sis. She's crying and carrying on.

F — I will not have you interfere with me! If you don't like it, you can get the hell out of here too!

GF — Look, son, don't worry, I'll scrape up some money and help you. (Grandmother cries, gets down on her knees to the Father and says: "Please, let's be reasonable. If you need some money, I'm sure Grandfather will help you." Father pushes Grandmother aside, slams the door and walks away.)

* * * * *

Another scene between Father and Sister

Father walks into the bedroom and finds his daughter on the bed, crying hysterically. He looks at her and says: "You are a fool! What the hell are you crying about? Who are you to butt into this matter?" The girl jumps out of bed, runs into the bathroom and slams the door. The Father knocks on the door and shouts: "Unlock this door and come out, or I'll break it down. Come out right now! You're just as crazy as your mother and brother. I'll put an end to all this. Your brother will go to work and there will be no school." She unlocks the door. Tears are rolling down her face. As she steps out of the bathroom, her father grabs her by the wrists, drags her into the bedroom and throws her on the bed. Again she screams hysterically and falls to the floor, just as the Mother walks in.

M — Oh, my darling, what has happened? (To F.) What have you done to her? (She also screams, cries hysterically and tries to pick up her daughter. But she cannot. The Father helps to put her into bed. The Mother takes

72

off the daughter's shoes and covers her. The daughter continues crying.)

M — (To F.) Get out of this room and leave her alone.

The Father refuses to go and says: "You get out of this room! What kind of a crazy family do I have?"

Then P comes into the room, followed by GF and GM. There is a big argument by all, with fussing, screaming and crying, until the son and Father have a scuffle.

The Father then rushes out of the bedroom and into the living room, followed by the GF and GM, while the Mother and P remain with the Sister in the bedroom. F is shaking with hostility and grief. GF and GM are pleading with him to give in to the boy, that they will get the money somehow and give it to the boy, so that F need not spend a penny for the boy's education. Sister remains in the bedroom while P goes into the living room and tells the Father: "I will go to college out of town whether you say so or not. I will work my way through school. The hell with you!" He starts to leave the room when the Father grabs him. P punches the Father in the face, then runs out of the room and out of the house.

The Mother comes back into the living room, sobbing, and sits near the GF and GM. She cannot look her husband in the face.

F — I am the boss of the house. I pay the bills and everyone in this house will do as I say, or else get out!

The Mother comes up to him, crying and pleading with him to go get the boy and bring him back into the house. She begs him to permit P to go to an out of town college for the first year. If he allows it, they will make it up to him in any way he demands.

F — Here you go again, spoiling your children, working against me, countermanding my best ideas and wrecking the family.

M — I am not wrecking the family. I am pleading with you to save the family. (The GF and GM rush out, endeavoring to find the son.)

D — I think we've had enough of this Psychodrama. Let us now hear from the audience. Will any one give an opinion, ask a question, make suggestions or any remarks about what they have witnessed?

A1 — Yes, I would like to know more about P's experience during his younger years.

D — I cannot reveal much of this, because it was told to me in confidence.

A2 — It seems to me that a strong factor in the psychodrama was the authoritarian father, who is more interested in his own ideas, and their acceptance, than what would bring the best results. Is it possible that the father was jealous of the son because the mother and other members of the family took the son's side and the mother and sister spoiled him? I also would like to know his previous experiences and background.

D — Yes, there is no doubt that if you would know the history of this young man and his family during his younger years, it would be easier to understand the situation here. There is no doubt that the father was too authoritarian and rigid. However, he may have had good reasons for part of his attitude. This young man does not

74

know how to study, and although he is finishing high school, he has shown no definite talent or desire for the kind of studies he is to pursue in college, and is only interested in TV, movies and escaping. The father did not give his reasons for wanting the boy in a city college, but I presume he wants the boy near-by because he thought if he were far away from home he might flunk out and get into trouble. The other members of the family indulged in the wishful thinking that the boy would study hard and make good.

It is also true that the mother did spoil him. She made no demands and permitted him to get away without doing any chores around the house. The mother did love the boy to excess.

The sister identified herself with the mother and imitated her.

The father was a strong authoritarian and was also strict with his daughter. The sister also identified herself with her brother. In the past, she too wanted to go to an out of town college, but was prohibited from leaving the state.

If you would know all the details, it would be easier to understand this psychodrama. However, we must come to a conclusion from what we have seen here tonight and from future psychodramas.

I can say this, that the father's father was also a strict disciplinarian and authoritarian. The mother's parents were easy going people. The father is rigid because his parents were also rigid, and the father had a very difficult childhood. He left school at the end of the second year of high school. Not because he flunked out, but because he had to go to work.

It is possible the father feels that the son has had too many opportunities and privileges, and feels: why should his son have the expensive experience of an out of town college when the father did not have such an opportunity? This might have made him hostile and jealous towards the boy. There is no doubt that the father resented the mother's catering to the boy. When they all ate together, the mother would always serve the boy first and give him the best or the largest portions. The father repeatedly asked the boy to carry out certain chores in the house, but the mother did it for him.

A3 — This psychodrama makes me think that the reasons for these actions are the results of an oedipal situation. This situation was brought out because of the background of the parents. The son was pushed into an oedipal situation. It also seems that it isn't a typical or classical oedipus affair, but it does smack of some remnants of it.

Yes, I agree. There are some of these elements which might have motivated such a picture. It is also true that the father has some points on his side, namely, that the boy was overprotected, was spoiled, and did not experience responsibilities and duties. It is likely, then, that when removed from his parents completely, he might become an unsuccessful student or get into trouble.

Some compromise situation should take place, like the son attending a near-by school, perhaps within the radius of under 100 miles, so that he could come home weekends or some weekends. This additional expense could be taken care of by the grandparents.

Perhaps the father should listen in on such psychodramas, or consult a psychiatrist or psychologist who may be able to soften him so that he can assume a softer role. If there will be no compromise, there may be further difficulties. A very good solution would be for the father and mother to attend a number of psychodramas, and to undergo psychotherapy or be psychoanalyzed. But this may be impractical, as the father does not believe in such things. We will see in our future psychodramas that we may discover other scenes, clues or detailed facts which will help us to arrive at definite conclusions.

These latter statements may seem reasonable to some, while others may take exception. The tentative suggestions may be useless if P will not follow up with future psychodramas and if the father is so rigid that he may not care to be bothered with such "trivialities."

This psychodrama continued for another five sessions. In the future, not only do we have to know more details, but we should try to work out the "teles" (or transferences) with the various cases and the reasons for them. This is a possibility in many cases, and helps us to understand better, in various ways, how to counsel or guide the protagonist and family.

At times, one psychodrama can be very helpful; at other times, repeated psychodramas may be needed to act out other scenes and clues for real benefits. Sometimes other forms of therapy may have to be added.

What the protagonist says, hears, feels and learns during these psychodramas, and his cathexis — his acting out spontaneously and by his own direction and that of others — all of this gives him confidence, methods for solving his problems, courage, insights and a better feeling.